Contents

Unit contents chart

4

Units 1-20

8

Tapescripts

88

Appendix 1 - irregular verbs

95

Appendix 2 - letter layout

96

Appendix 3 - common telex abbreviations

97

Multilingual word list

98

Unit contents chart

1 **People in tourism**

Present simple for facts and habits; present continuous for temporary activities.

Finding out about people working in tourism. Listening for specific information. Writing a job description.

2 **Flight reservations**

Requests: *Can ...?/Could ...?/Would ...?*; *have got*.

Dealing with flight reservations. Understanding abbreviations and symbols. Days and dates.

3 **Changes and cancellations**

Wh- questions; present continuous for future arrangements.

Making alterations to flight bookings. Asking for and giving factual information. Writing letters explaining cancellation charges.

4 **Rail enquiries**

would like + to infinitive, *would like + nouns*; countable and uncountable nouns.

Dealing with enquiries about rail travel. Reading a descriptive passage. Writing replies to requests for information.

5 **Timetables**

Preferences: *would prefer (to)/would rather*.

Answering timetable enquiries on the telephone. Using the 12-hour/24-hour clock. Inferring meaning from context.

6

Travel requirements

Degrees of obligation: *must/have to, needn't, mustn't.*

Informing customers about travel requirements. Transferring information from a letter to a form. Writing letters of confirmation.

7

Giving directions

Imperatives in instructions; prepositions of place and movement.

Understanding and giving directions on a map and in an airport building. Reading for specific details. Talking about services and facilities.

8

Tourist information

Giving advice and making suggestions: *should, ought to.*

Offering advice to tourists. Listening for specific information. Reading and writing promotional material.

9

Methods of payment

Past tense of regular and irregular verbs.

Dealing with different methods of payment. Listening and transferring information to a form. Writing a narrative in the past simple.

10

Hotel facilities (1)

Comparatives and superlatives: *-er, -est; more ... than, the most ...*

Comparing hotel facilities. Listening and inferring. Writing brochure descriptions of hotel services.

Unit contents chart

11 *Hotel facilities (2)*

Talking about plans and intentions: *be going to.*

Visiting hotels as a tour company representative. Reading promotional material. Writing letters of recommendation.

12 *Telephone enquiries*

will; telephone language; time prepositions.

Taking reservations over the telephone. A guide to telephone language and behaviour. Writing telephone messages and letters of confirmation.

13 *Checking in*

Degrees of probability : sentences with *if* and *when.*

Receiving guests. Reading and talking about features of the hotel industry. Understanding and writing telexes. Promoting your country's hotel industry.

14 *Complaints*

Expressions used when complaining or apologizing; tense revision.

Dealing with complaints. Building dialogues. Guidance on replying to letters of complaint.

15 *Conference facilities*

enough/too with nouns and adjectives.

Describing conference requirements and facilities. Promoting your town/region as a conference centre. Organizing a conference.

E N G **M**

◆ Trish Stott & Roger Holt ◆

O X F O   P R E S S

This book is dedicated to
Dan, Josh, Dick, and Mary

16 Local tours

Present and past passive.

Describing processes. Reading and contrasting texts. Discussion about the effects of tourism in your country. Preparing and giving a talk.

17 Foreign tours

Present simple for programmes and schedules.

Explaining tour diaries. Reading about special interest holidays. Using descriptive adjectives. Preparing and writing tour diaries.

18 Itineraries

Present perfect for talking about experiences; present perfect contrasted with past simple.

Dealing with enquiries about itineraries. Planning and writing personal itineraries. Controlled dialogue building.

19 Car and equipment hire

Present perfect with *for* and *since*.

Arranging car and equipment hire. Describing sports facilities and advising clients on choosing a resort.

20 Job interviews

Degrees of probability: the conditional with *would*.

Taking part in job interviews. Reading and writing letters of application. Discussion on the future of the tourist industry.

Reading

Read these magazine extracts and decide which job you think is the most interesting. Discuss your reasons with the rest of the class.

Marie Blanc works in a large travel agency in Paris. English is her only foreign language.

'I was born in Paris and I'm very happy here. But I like this job because I'm interested in travel. On the whole, this agency deals with business customers. I arrange their flights and hotel bookings all over the world. Apart from that, we often get foreign tourists who want to change their travel arrangements. Of course English is essential.

The best thing about this job? I get cheap holidays!'

Manuel Romero works in the Tourist Information Office at Malaga airport in the south of Spain. He speaks English and a little French.

'Most of the tourists who come here are British, but we also have a lot of Dutch and Germans. They usually come on package holidays, so everything is organized in advance. But sometimes they want to hire a car or do something a bit different. Then I give them advice. They usually don't know any Spanish, apart from "Olé", so I use my English all the time.

It's an interesting job and some of the people I meet are very funny. One American couple asked if they could fly to Torremolinos. That's only about ten kilometres from here!'

Paola Conti is a tour guide in Florence. She speaks English and Spanish.

'I take groups of English speakers – Americans, English, Australians – on bus tours of Florence. In the summer there are four different tours and every time I go out somebody asks a new question, so I never get bored. Anyway, I'd hate to work in an office. I don't want to do this for the rest of my life, but I'm enjoying the job at the moment and I earn a lot of money in the summer.'

Language study 1

We use the present simple to talk about facts (they stay the same for a long time) and habits (they happen again and again).

Facts: *Maria Blanc **works** in a travel agency. This agency **deals** mainly with business customers.*

Habits: *Every time **I go** out somebody asks a new question. They usually **come** on package holidays.*

Practice A

Make sentences from these prompts. The first one has been done for you.

Example: sometimes/want to/hire/car (They)
They sometimes want to hire a car.

1 earn/a lot of/money/summer (Paola)
2 speak/English/French (Manuel)
3 never/get/bored (Paola)
4 not/work/Tourist Information Office (Marie)
5 live/Malaga (Manuel)
6 not/get/cheap holidays (Paola and Manuel)
7 all/speak/English (We)

Practice B

Now find out about your partner.

Student A
Ask questions starting *Do you . . .?* using the prompts below.

Student B
Answer the questions with *Yes, I do.* or *No, I don't.*

1 get up early/every day?
2 work/travel agency?
3 often/watch/TV?
4 speak/Portuguese?
5 sometimes/drink/wine?
6 smoke?

Now ask another student about his/her partner.

Example: *Does she smoke?   Yes, she does.*
No, she doesn't.

Practice C

Write down ten things you *never/sometimes/usually/often/always* do in a normal day. Tell your partner about them.

Examples: *I never eat breakfast.*
I usually watch TV.

Listening

Listen to this man talking about his job. Put a tick beside the correct picture.

Now listen again. Look at these questions, then complete the answers.

A What does he do?
B He teaches . . .
A What is he teaching the group about at the moment?
B He's teaching them about . . .
A What are the people in the group doing?
B They . . .

Language study 2

Remember that we use the present simple tense to talk about facts and habits.

*She **works** in a bank.*
*They **play** golf every day.*

We use the present continuous tense to talk about activities happening now.

*She's **diving** at the moment.*

Practice D

Write the correct form of the verb in the space provided.

1   I ... (stay) in Paris this week, but I ... (usually/ live) in Madrid.
2   What ... (you/do)?
    I'm a tour guide. But I ...(only/work) in the summer.
3   Look! Those people ... (learn) to ski.
4   I ... (often/play) golf at the weekend.
5   Only a few British people ... (understand) Spanish.
6   Listen! What language ... (that man/speak)?
7   Mario ... (speak) three languages.
8   What ... (you/do)?
    I ... (wait) for a bus.

Practice E

Look at the pictures. Work with a partner. Ask and answer questions.

Examples: *What does he do?*
                What are they doing?

Activity

Work in pairs. Take turns to be **A** and **B**.

Student A
Choose a job. Do not tell your partner what it is!
Answer only *Yes* or *No* to your partner's questions.

Student B
Try to find out what your partner's job is. You may ask questions, but only questions starting *Do you . . .?*

Example: *Do you work in an office?*

How many questions did you have to ask? Try again using different jobs.

Writing

Look at the notes below about John Hunter.

```
Background information

Name:        John Hunter

Job:         Representative for
             CampHols

Place:       Corinthia, Austria

Languages:   English only


The job

Welcomes new campers; gives
advice on places to visit and
things to do; keeps the
campsite clean.

Doesn't get much money but has
plenty of free time; sometimes
gets a bit lonely, but meets a
lot of interesting people.
```

Imagine you are John Hunter. Now write about your job.

My name is John Hunter. I work . . .

Summary

Now you can

▦ Talk about people in tourism . . .
tourist information officer, travel agent, tour guide, windsurfing instructor

▦ Talk about habits . . .
They usually come on package holidays.
Every time I go out somebody asks a new question.

▦ . . . and facts
Paola Conti speaks Italian, English, and Spanish.
Manuel Romero works at Malaga airport.

▦ Talk about temporary states and activities
I'm enjoying the job at the moment.
At the moment I'm teaching them about . . .

New words

advice	foreign
arrange	instructor
arrangement	organized
booking	package holiday
business	representative
campsite	scuba diving
camper	tour guide
customer	travel agency
deal with	welcome
flight	windsurfing

Listening

Listen to the conversation between an English tourist and the travel clerk in a Barcelona travel agency. As you listen decide if the sentences below are true or false. If a sentence is false, write the correct answer.

1   The tourist wants a flight from Barcelona to Rome.
2   He wants to travel on Monday.
3   There are restrictions on the ticket.
4   The man's telephone number in Barcelona is 2018440.
5   The flight leaves in the morning.
6   Check-in time is at half past seven.

Language study 1

Polite/formal requests

__Could__ you wait a minute while I check availability?
__Would__ you please check in an hour before departure?

Informal requests

__Can__ you give me your contact address?

Practice A

The words in the travel agent's questions below are in the wrong order. Write them out in the correct order and match them with the right customer's response.

1 ticket you show please me your can?
2 sign you form could this please?
3 have telephone can number your I?
4 check at would 8.30 please p.m. in you?
5 earlier you an could flight take?

a Certainly. May I borrow your pen?
b Yes, it's 2018550.
c But that's two hours before departure!
d I'm afraid not. I can't get to the airport before 3 p.m.
e Yes. Here it is.

Now practise these dialogues with a partner. Take turns to be the travel agent and the customer.

Practice B

Work in pairs, one as the boss, the other as the secretary.

Boss
Use the suggestions below to make questions starting *Can*, *Could*, and *Would*.

Secretary
Say *Yes* or *No* politely.

Example: type/letter

Boss   *Would you type this letter, please?*
Secretary   *Yes, certainly.*
        or   *I'm afraid I'm rather busy at present. Could I do it later?*

1 make/telephone call to . . .
2 send/telex to . . .
3 bring/coffee
4 come/my office
5 book/flight to . . .
6 make/hotel reservation
7 cancel/appointment with . . .

Language study 2

In British English we often use *have got* to talk about possession, relationships, etc. *I have got* means exactly the same as *I have*.

I've got an open round-the-world ticket.
Have you **got** your ticket with you?

Practice C

Complete the statements and questions below using *have got*.

Example: . . . his passport and ticket? (he)
        Has he got his passport and ticket?

1 . . . a very good brochure on Italy. (they)
2 . . . a return ticket? (your son)
3 . . . a room facing the sea? (I)
4 . . . a swimming-pool. (the hotel)
5 . . . an expiry date? (these tickets)
6 . . . a stopover in Singapore. (we)

Practice D

Here are four things your partner might have:

Write down four more things. Now take turns to ask and answer questions.

Example: **A**   *Have you got . . .?*
        B   *Yes, I have./No, I haven't.*

Flight reservations

Reading

Look at this extract from the Air France timetable
and at the key to the abbreviations and symbols.

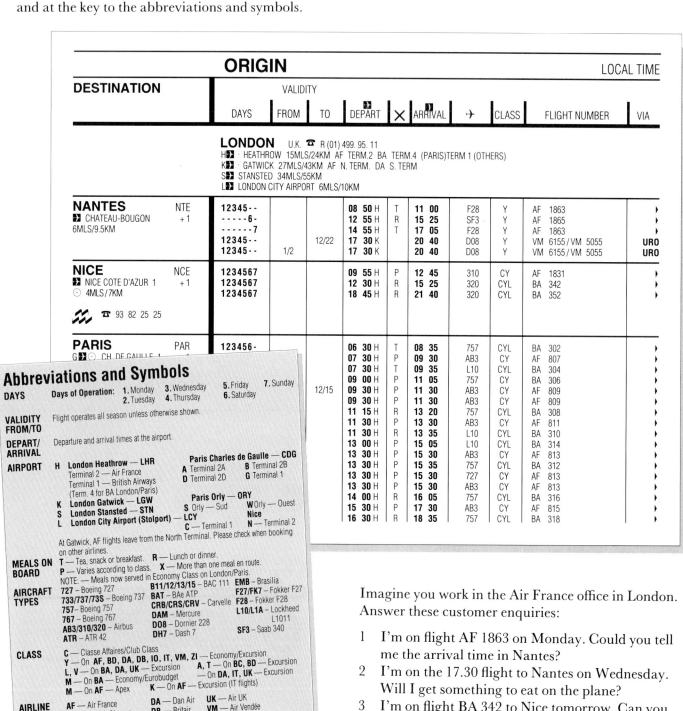

Imagine you work in the Air France office in London.
Answer these customer enquiries:

1 I'm on flight AF 1863 on Monday. Could you tell
me the arrival time in Nantes?

2 I'm on the 17.30 flight to Nantes on Wednesday.
Will I get something to eat on the plane?

3 I'm on flight BA 342 to Nice tomorrow. Can you
tell me which airport that leaves from?

4 Can I fly Club Class to Nantes?

5 Is flight VM 6155 to Nantes non-stop?

Now write down three similar enquiries. Ask your
partner for the information you want.

Days and dates

Listen to the cassette and repeat. Check your pronunciation.

1 Thursday, 1st February
2 Wednesday, 25th July
3 Tuesday, 3rd April
4 Sunday, 7th January
5 Saturday, 12th May
6 Friday, 2nd March
7 Tuesday, 11th September
8 Thursday, 30th August
9 Monday, 13th November
10 Friday, 26th October
11 Monday, 18th June
12 Wednesday, 19th December

What important dates do you have in *your* year? Tell a partner about them.

birthdays/holidays/examinations/special occasions

Example: *My birthday is on 26th May.*

Activity

Listen again to the conversation on the cassette. With a partner write out a dialogue between a travel agent and a tourist. You may want to use the expressions from **Language study 1** and **2**.

Travel agent
You work in a travel agency in London. Help the tourist to arrange the flight he/she wants. Use the information in the Air France timetable.

Tourist
You want to fly to Nantes. Ask the travel agent to arrange your flight. Find out about different flights.

Useful expressions:

☐ *When would you like to travel?*
☐ *There may be some restrictions.*
☐ *The flight leaves at . . .*
☐ *Have a good flight!*

Now practise the dialogue with your partner.

Summary

Now you can

▪ Make polite requests
Could you give me your contact address and telephone number?
Would you please check in an hour before departure?

▪ Take travel reservations
When would you like to travel?
Have you got your ticket with you?

New words

airline	non-stop
appointment	operate
availability	reservation
brochure	restriction
cancel	return
check-in	round-the-world
check in	stopover
computer	telex
contact address	timetable
departure	travel clerk
expiry date	

Listening

Listen to the telephone conversation between a
Swedish businessman who wants to change a
reservation, and a travel agent in Bangkok. Now
complete this ticket:

PASSENGER TICKET AND BAGGAGE CHECK SUBJECT TO CONDITIONS CONTAINED IN THIS TICKET ISSUED BY THAI INTERNATIONAL	CONJUNCTION TICKET(S)						
PASSENGER NAME			NOT TRANSFERABLE BOOKING REFERENCE		ORIGIN/DESTINATION BKK/NRT		AGENT CPN
					BOOKING REFERENCE Q		
					ISSUED IN EXCHANGE FOR		

X/O	DESTINATION	CARRIER	CLASS	FLIGHT	DATE	TIME	STATUS	FARE BASIS/TKT. DESIGNATOR	NOT VALID BEFORE	NOT VALID AFTER
TO	VOID									
TO	VOID					VOID				
TO	VOID					VOID				
TO	BANGKOK	TG	Y			VOID				
						OK Y				

FARE THB 22415	FARE CALCULATION	BAGGAGE CHECKED UNCHECKED	PCS.	WT.	UNCHECKED	PCS.	WT.	UNCHECKED	PCS.	WT.	UNCHECKED	PCS.	WT.

EQUIV. FARE PAID

16APR91BKK TG(EH)TYO M565.16P TYOBKK317.28NUC882.44
END ROE 25.39944THB22415

TAX

TAX

TOTAL

FORM OF PAYMENT
AGT/NON REF

A/L-AGT. INFO

ORIGINAL ISSUE

TOUR CODE

Language study 1

Look at how these questions are formed.

What's your name, please?
Where are you flying to?
Which flight are you on?
What's the flight number?
When do you want to fly?

Practice A

Match the following questions and answers.

1 Which airline are you travelling with?
2 What's your name, please?
3 When do I check in?
4 Where are you going?
5 What date is your flight?
6 Which airport do I leave from?
7 What day is that?
8 Where would you like to sit?
9 Which class, madam?

a To New York.
b Heathrow.
c Business class.
d One hour before departure.
e By the window, please.
f Greta Scala.
g Air France.
h Thursday.
i 22nd June.

Practice B

Put the words in these questions in the correct order.

1 time the leave what flight does?
2 arrive London do when in you?
3 are hotel which in you staying?
4 to would on you where holiday like go?
5 number your what contact is telephone?
6 you travel like Tokyo to when would to?
7 Tuesdays which Madrid on airlines to fly?
8 your going brother is where in March to?

Practice C

Make questions with *What*, *When*, *Where*, and *Which*, using the following prompts. Then ask your partner the questions.

1 live?
2 date/birthday?
3 time/go to bed?
4 favourite food?
5 would like/go/on holiday?
6 languages/can/speak?
7 job/would like/do?
8 would like/work?

Language study 2

We often use the present continuous to talk or ask about arrangements in the future.

Where **are** *you* **flying** *to?*
I'm **staying** *with friends.*

Practice D

Fill the gaps in this dialogue with the correct form of the verb.

A Where . . . (go) on holiday this summer?
B I . . . (go) to Bermuda with some friends.
A Great! How long . . . (stay)?
B Three weeks.
A Wow! It sounds expensive!
B Not really. I . . . (not/pay) for the flight.
A I see! Now I know why you like working in a travel agency!

Practise the completed dialogue with a partner.

Practice E

Fill in your diary for next weekend using the prompts below. Leave some times blank. Don't show it to your partner!

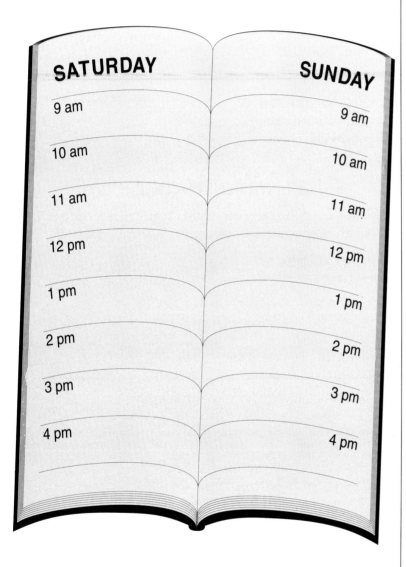

SATURDAY

9 am

10 am

11 am

12 pm

1 pm

2 pm

3 pm

4 pm

SUNDAY

9 am

10 am

11 am

12 pm

1 pm

2 pm

3 pm

4 pm

write some letters/go shopping/visit a friend/play tennis/go to the cinema/make an important telephone call/wash your hair/go to a party/have lunch with a friend/go to church/study English/paint your bedroom

Now try to arrange to meet your partner. Take turns to ask:

What are you doing at . . . on . . .?

Reading and writing

Study the cancellation and alteration conditions below. Then read the letter from Mr Clark and complete the reply.

must be made at the time of booking in order to secure the reservation.

8. CANCELLATIONS
If you have to cancel your holiday, please inform us in writing immediately. Cancellation charges are as follows:

More than 42 days ....deposit
29-42 days.........................40% of holiday cost
15-28 days.........................65% of holiday cost
14 days - day of departure ......100% of holiday
cost

9. BOOKING ALTERATIONS
If you wish to make any amendment to your booking after it has been confirmed, there will be a charge of £15 per booking to cover our administration costs.

10. TRAVEL INSURANCE
It is a requirement when booking your holiday

87 Ridgeton Avenue,
London W9 1BB.

Skyhigh Travel,
17 Dingley Court,
London.

17 May 1991

Dear Sir,

Holiday to Turkey, 1-15 July 1991

Unfortunately owing to illness we may have to cancel our holiday plans this year. Is there a charge if we cancel before the end of May? We would also like to know about any amendment charge if we can change the dates of our booking.

Yours faithfully,

Steve Clark

Steven Clark

Now write a reply to the following letter. You are Mr Harper.

See Appendix 2 for an explanation of letter layout.

Activity

Listen to the cassette again. Now try to have a similar telephone conversation with a partner (if possible, sit back to back). Use the suggestions below.

Useful expressions:

☐ *Good morning. . . . Travel. Can I help you?*
☐ *I'll just check availability.*
☐ *You're welcome.*
☐ *Thank you for calling.*

Customer

Imagine you want to change a flight booking. Write down your destination, flight number, and departure date. You want to travel at the same time and on the same flight, but one week earlier. Phone Skyhigh Travel and explain.

Travel agent

You work for Skyhigh Travel. You receive a call from a customer who wants to alter a ticket. Find out the person's name, destination, and flight number. Ask when the customer wants to fly. Arrange the alteration.

Summary

Now you can

▪ Ask wh- questions
  Where are you flying to?
  When do you want to fly?

▪ Deal with changes and cancellations
  Would you like me to change . . .?
  There will be a charge of £15 per booking.

▪ Write letters about changes and cancellations

New words

administration costs	deposit
alter	destination
alteration	Economy Class
amendment	flight number
cancellation charge	manager
confirmed	passenger
cover	via

Listening

An Australian tourist is asking a Spanish travel agent about rail travel in Britain. Read the questions below.

1   What is the tourist planning to do with his wife and son?
2   How does the BritRail Pass work?
3   Do all children travel free on British Rail?

Now listen to the cassette and answer the questions.

Language study 1

We use *would like* for polite requests and offers.

would like + noun
would like + *to* infinitive

I'd like *some information on rail travel in the UK.*
Would *you* **like** *to take a seat?*
I'd like *to know about tickets.*

Practice A

Make dialogues like this using the suggestions below.

Example: **A**   *Would you like to speak to Mr Smith?*
               B   *No, I'd like to speak to Mrs Brown, please.*

1   make a reservation/an enquiry
2   leave this morning/this afternoon
3   pay by cheque/credit card

Practice B

Now do the same using these suggestions.

Example: **A**   *Would you like a return?*
               B   *No, I'd like a single, please.*

1   an aisle seat/a window seat
2   smoking/non-smoking
3   first class/standard class

Practice C

Complete the sentences below with *would like* or *would like to*.

1   I . . . reserve a seat on the 17.45 to London, please.
2   We . . . two BritRail Passes, please.
3   . . . you . . . a single or a return?
4   My husband . . . travel tomorrow.
5   . . . you . . . look at this brochure?
6   British Rail . . . apologize for the late arrival of this train.
7   I . . . a return ticket to Rome, please.
8   Mrs Badini . . . more details about rail travel in the UK.

Now think of six things you would like to do. Tell your partner about them.

Example: *I'd like to work in New York.*

Language study 2

We use *a* meaning *one* with countable nouns (e.g. tourist, ticket, discount).

We use *some* with uncountable nouns (e.g. information, luggage, news).

*Is there **a** discount for children?*
*I'd like **some** information on rail travel.*

Practice D

Fill in the gaps in these sentences using *a* or *some*.

1   Can I buy . . . BritRail Pass in Barcelona?
2   Is there . . . discount for children?
3   Can I have . . . information about flights to Australia?
4   She's got . . . week's holiday in Spain.
5   They've got . . . luggage on the train.
6   I'd like . . . advice about hotels.
7   Here is . . . news about flight departures.
8   We get . . . homework every night.
9   Can I have . . . change for the telephone, please?
10 There is . . . buffet car on the train.

Practice E

Can you think of other examples of countable and uncountable nouns? Make two lists. Compare your lists with your partner's. Now check them with your teacher.

Reading

1   Read the passage on the right carefully. Then write four sentences about the text. Try to use your own words. Make some of the sentences true and some of them false. Then test your partner.
2   Underline all the adjectives in the passage and make sure you understand them. You may use a dictionary.
3   Would you like to go on this kind of holiday? Discuss your answer with your partner.

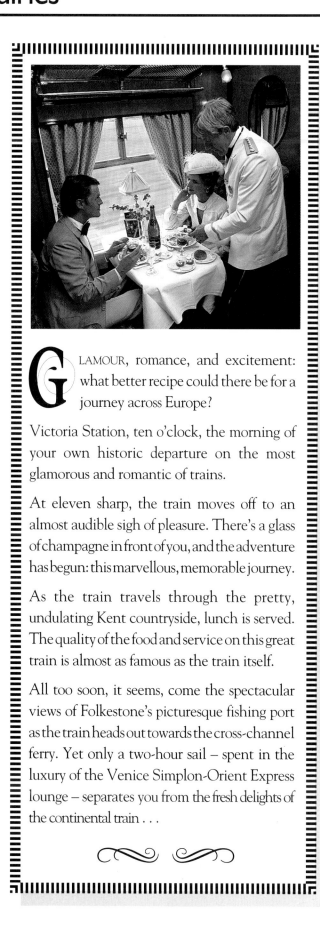

GLAMOUR, romance, and excitement: what better recipe could there be for a journey across Europe?

Victoria Station, ten o'clock, the morning of your own historic departure on the most glamorous and romantic of trains.

At eleven sharp, the train moves off to an almost audible sigh of pleasure. There's a glass of champagne in front of you, and the adventure has begun: this marvellous, memorable journey.

As the train travels through the pretty, undulating Kent countryside, lunch is served. The quality of the food and service on this great train is almost as famous as the train itself.

All too soon, it seems, come the spectacular views of Folkestone's picturesque fishing port as the train heads out towards the cross-channel ferry. Yet only a two-hour sail – spent in the luxury of the Venice Simplon-Orient Express lounge – separates you from the fresh delights of the continental train . . .

Activity

With a partner take turns to be a tourist and an SNCF agent.

Tourist

You have a wife and a child aged six. You are considering a two-week holiday travelling around France by train. Ask about the France Vacances Pass. Find out:

> how much it costs.
> how long the Pass lasts.
> what is included.
> how far you can travel.
> if you can use it every day.
> about the reduced rate for your child.

SNCF agent

Look at the information from the Liberté brochure on the France Vacances Pass and answer the tourist's questions.

Useful expressions:

☐ *I recommend you buy . . .*
☐ *I suggest . . .*

LIBERTÉ
FROM JUST £279 INCLUSIVE

HERE'S WHAT YOU GET

A **"France Vacances Pass" railrover** valid 15 days and offering you unlimited 2nd class rail travel on any 4 days during that period. Remember, France has the largest rail network in Western Europe with fast comfortable trains which will take you to virtually every part of the country. TGVs, of course, are the fastest trains in the world running at up to 300km/h. Your "France Vacances Pass" also entitles you to many bonuses and discounts, including reduced rate car hire in around 200 stations.

Vouchers for 7 nights' accommodation with breakfast and dinner* in a countrywide network of over 140 selected family hotels. All guarantee a high standard of comfort and service and, since each one is individually owned and run, you get personal attention and authentic regional cuisine – the true flavour of traditional French hospitality.

The price of your holiday includes accommodation based on shared occupancy of a double / twin room.

*Bed and Breakfast in Paris and Cannes.

PRICES - per person

	BASIC PACKAGE
LOW: Until 29th June and from 15th September	£279
HIGH: From 30th June to 14th September	£299

CHILDREN FROM 4 to 11 YRS

CHILD SHARING A ROOM WITH PARENTS	
One child	£50

Writing

Read this letter and use the notes below to complete the reply.

40 Walton Crescent,
Oxford OX2 6DP.

French Railways Ltd.,
179 Piccadilly,
London W1V OBA.

12 April 1991.

Dear Sir,
    I would like some information on rail travel in France. I am planning to spend some time there in August with my wife and son (aged 10).
    We would really like to travel all over France. Are there any all-inclusive tickets?

Yours faithfully,

John Prentice.

Notes for reply

Paragraph 1:   Thank the writer for his letter.

Paragraph 2:   Recommend the France Vacances Pass.
Explain how it works and what it includes.
Mention the price for adults and for a child sharing with parents.

Paragraph 3:   Mention that you are enclosing the leaflet.
Invite the writer to contact you for further information.

---

17 April 1991

Dear Mr Prentice

(1) Thank you for . . .

(2) I recommend that you buy . . .

(3) I enclose . . . Please do not hesitate to . . .

Yours sincerely

See Appendix 2 for an explanation of letter layout.

Summary

Now you can

▨ Deal with travel enquiries
I'd like some information on rail travel in the UK.
I recommend you buy a BritRail Pass.
I suggest you buy them in the UK.

▨ Recognize countable and uncountable nouns
Is there a discount for children?
Can I have some information about . . .?

New words

adult	enquiry
adventure	ferry
aisle	included
apologize	leaflet
buffet car	luggage
cheque	network
continental	offer
countryside	recommend
credit card	reduced rate
cross-channel	request
discount	single
enclose	unlimited

Listening

Look at the Amsterdam to Paris timetable. Then listen to the telephone conversation.

1   What time does the man have to be in Paris?
2   Which train does the man decide to take?
3   Why doesn't he want to take the 12.26 departure?

AMSTERDAM - BRUSSELS - PARIS

Amsterdam dep.	...	....	0622	0700	0724	0826	0853	0926	1026	1050	1226	....	1326	....	1426	....	1526	1553	1726	....	1826	1926	2026	2215
Schipol dep.	...	....	0642	|	0742	0844	|	0944	1044	|	1244	....	1344	....	1444	....	1544	|	1744	....	1844	1944	2044	|
Den Haag dep.	...	....	0712	0742	0810	0912	0934	1012	1112	1135	1312	....	1412	....	1512	....	1612	1636	1812	....	1912	2012	2112	2307
Rotterdam dep.	...	....	0731	0806	0831	0931	0954	1031	1131	1204	1331	....	1431	....	1531	....	1631	1658	1831	....	1931	2031	2131	2334
Roosendaal dep.	...	....	0814	0848	0914	1014	1032	1114	1214	1247	1414	....	1514	....	1614	....	1714	1743	1914	....	2014	2114	2214	0025
Antwerpen (Central) { arr.	...	....	0843	|	0943	1043	|	1143	1243	|	1443	....	1543	....	1643	....	1743	|	1943	....	2043	2143	2243	|
dep.	...	....	0849	|	0949	1049	|	1149	1249	|	1449	....	1549	....	1649	....	1749	|	1949	....	2049	2149	2249	|
Antwerpen-Berchem dep.	...	....	0853	0917	0953	1053	1059	1153	1253	1315	1453	....	1553	....	1653	....	1753	1812	1953	....	2053	2153	2253	0054
Brussels (Nord) { arr.	...	....	0921	0949	1021	1121	1130	1221	1321	1346	1521	....	1621	....	1721	....	1821	1843	2021	....	2121	2221	2321	0125
dep.	...	0758	0923	0951	1023	1123	1132	1223	1323	1349	1523	1551	1623	....	1723	....	1823	1845	2023	....	2123	2223	2323	0127
Brussels (Central) dep.	....	|	0927	|	1027	1127	|	1227	1327	|	1527	|	1627	....	1727	....	1827	|	2027	....	2127	2227	2327	|
Brussels (Midi) { arr.	...	0804	0930	0956	1030	1130	1137	1230	1330	1354	1530	1556	1630	....	1730	....	1830	1850	2030	....	2130	2230	2330	0134
dep.	0710	0810	....	1010	....	....	1149	....	....	1407	....	1610	....	1710	....	1810	....	1910	—	2041	....	....	....	0153
Mons dep.	....	0844	....	1044	....	....	....	....	1442	....	1644	....	....	|	....	1944	....	2116	....	....	....	0229		
St. Quentin dep.	....	....	1141	....	....	|	....	....	1540	....	1737	....	1931	....	2050	....	|	....	....	....	0441			
Paris (Nord) arr.	|	0936	1054	....	1254	....	....	1419	....	....	1705	....	1857	....	1940	....	2044	....	2206	....	2317	....	....	....	0625

Language study 1

Preferences

would rather (not) + infinitive without *to*

would prefer (not) + | *to* infinitive
| noun

*I'd **rather** not change.*
*I'd **prefer** to leave a bit later.*
*I'd **prefer** a later departure.*

Practice A

First answer these questions yourself. Then compare your answers with others in your class. Discuss the reasons for your answers.

1   Would you rather work in your country or abroad?
2   Would you prefer to be rich or famous?
3   Would you rather live alone or with your family?
4   Would you prefer to visit the USA or Britain?

Now write four similar questions to ask your partner. Take turns to ask and answer.

Practice B

Use the prompts below to make similar dialogues. Take turns to ask and answer.

Example: tea/coffee?
          A   *Would you rather have tea or coffee?*
          B   *I'd prefer tea, please.*

1   an afternoon departure/an evening departure?
2   smoking/non-smoking?
3   a window seat/an aisle seat?
4   a rear-facing seat/a front-facing seat?

Practice C

Fill the gaps in the dialogue with the correct form of the verb given.

A   Can I help you?
B   Yes. I ... (like) reserve a seat on the 10.15 a.m. train to London.
A   Certainly, sir. ... (prefer) smoking or non-smoking?
B   Non-smoking, please.
A   And ... (rather) have a window seat or an aisle seat?
B   I ... (prefer) a window seat, please.

Now practise the dialogue with a partner.

Language study 2

Timetables use the 24-hour clock to help prevent confusion, but we usually use the 12-hour clock when we speak.

18.57 becomes *three minutes to seven in the evening*
or *six fifty-seven p.m.*

Practice D

If possible, sit back to back with a partner. Take it in turns to be rail clerk and traveller on the telephone. Look at the timetable. Ask and answer questions about trains from Amsterdam to Brussels. Start with the 10.26 departure.

Example: **A** *What time does the 10.26 from Amsterdam arrive in Brussels?*
B *At 13.30.*
A *That's one thirty p.m., isn't it?*
B *Yes, sir/madam.*

Reading

Read the text and decide if the sentences which follow are true or false.

THE JOURNEY OF A NIGHT TIME

When travelling long distances (especially to and from Scotland) why not take an InterCity Sleeper and enjoy the luxury of sleeping en route? Whether for a business or leisure trip, Sleepers save you a day and yet offer a comfortable and convenient journey.

A FIRST CLASS EXPERIENCE

All cabins are fully air conditioned with integral washing facilities. Refreshments are available from the sleeper attendant who is always on hand to provide you with first class assistance. If you travel First Class on the routes between London and Edinburgh, Glasgow, Inverness or Aberdeen, and between Glasgow or Edinburgh and Plymouth most trains have the sleeper lounge service. You can enjoy a relaxing drink or light snack in the evenings and sit down to a cooked breakfast the following morning. Many of the First Class sleeper vehicles have now been refurbished providing new wider mattresses, quieter air-conditioning and brand new carpets and bedding.

EASY TO BOOK - EVEN EASIER TO TRAVEL

If you have the Standard ticket you can book a berth in a two berth sleeper cabin for just £20. If you hold a First Class ticket you can take a single berth cabin for just £22. A comfortable price to pay for a great night's rest.
For business travellers from Scotland special inclusive Scottish Executive tickets offering the option of sleeper travel in with the price of the ticket are available to many destinations in England. To book simply call at any main British Rail station, Travel Centre or British Rail appointed travel agent, or ring the Sleeper Reservations Office shown on the back page.

MOTORAIL

Why not take your car on the train? Full details of the services on which this facility is available can be found in the Motorail brochure available from all stations.
Until 31 March you can take your car on any InterCity Motorail service for as little as £10 on top of your own fare. Pick up the special leaflet for full details.

1 Only first class passengers may use the sleeper lounge service.
2 Only Scottish business travellers have the option of buying tickets with inclusive sleeper travel.
3 Until 31 March passengers can take a car on any InterCity Motorail service for £10.00.

Now look at the words below. Choose the best definition for each word in the context of the passage.

4 *leisure*   a work
           b relaxation
           c pleasure

5 *integral*   a basic
           b built-in
           c luxury

6 *on hand*   a available
           b happy
           c helping

7 *refurbished* a redecorated
           b made bigger
           c replaced

Activity

Listen again to the telephone dialogue. Now make a similar conversation between a rail employee and a traveller.

Rail employee
You work for Netherlands Railways in Rotterdam. Use the timetable at the start of the unit to answer the telephone enquiry.

Traveller
You are in Rotterdam. You want to travel to Paris tomorrow. Telephone Netherlands Railways and find out about trains. You must be in Paris by 9.00 p.m. at the latest. You can't leave Rotterdam before 1.00 p.m. You would prefer a direct train.

Useful expressions:

☐ *International Enquiries. Can I help you?*
☐ *Hold the line, please.*
☐ *There's an express at . . .*

Summary

Now you can

▪ Give information about trains and train times
  You have to change at Brussels.
  The 12.26 arrives in Paris at 18.57.

▪ Talk and ask about preferences
  I'd rather not change.
  Would you prefer smoking or non-smoking?

▪ Convert the 24-hour clock to the 12-hour clock
  13.30 or 1.30 p.m.
      half past one in the afternoon.

New words

abroad	prefer
assistance	preference
direct	prevent
employee	rear-facing
front-facing	refreshments
inclusive	sleeper

Listening

First fill the gaps in this dialogue with the words below. Use each word or expression once.

cost/price/needn't/I have to/interested/includes/ You have to/accommodation/provisional

Customer: Good morning. I'm . . . in the 16-night Classical Tour of India. How much does it . . .?

Travel agent: When would you like to go?

Customer: February.

Travel agent: February. Let me see – the . . . is £1573 for 16 nights.

Customer: Are internal flights included?

Travel agent: Yes. The price . . . the return flight, internal flights in India, all airport taxes, transfers to and from the hotel, and the hotel . . . itself.

Customer: Do . . . pay extra for a single room?

Travel agent: Yes, sir. There's a single-room supplement of £20 a night.

Customer: What about visas?

Travel agent: . . . have a visa for India and Nepal. I suggest you apply as soon as you book the holiday.

Customer: When do I have to confirm? Can I make a . . . booking?

Travel agent: You . . . confirm straight away. I can keep an option open on the holiday for seven days. But after that you must confirm and pay a deposit. The balance is due eight weeks before departure.

Now listen to the conversation and check your answers.

Language study

Obligation

We use *must* and *have to* to indicate obligation.

*After that you **must** confirm and pay a deposit.*
*You **have to** have a visa for India.*

No obligation

We use *don't have to*, *don't need to*, and *needn't* to show lack of obligation.

*You **needn't** confirm straight away.* (It is not necessary.)

Prohibition

We use *must not* to indicate that something is not allowed.

*You **must not** smoke during take-off.* (Do not smoke!)

Practice A

Complete these sentences using *must*, *have to*, *needn't* or *don't have to*.

1 You ... confirm today. I can keep the option open for seven days.
2 You ... pay the balance eight weeks before departure.
3 You ... pay the whole amount now, just a deposit.
4 When you receive your final invoice you ... pay immediately.
5 You ... check in an hour before departure.
6 You ... buy a seat reservation for trains in England but we recommend it at weekends.
7 You ... carry a passport for internal travel.
8 You ... inform us about cancellations in writing.

Practice B

Here are some facts about Britain in note form. Write sentences like this:

Example: be 18 to vote/to get married
You must be 18 to vote, but you needn't be 18 to get married.

1 have a licence to drive a car/to ride a bike.
2 be over 16 to buy cigarettes/to smoke.
3 make flight reservations/train reservations.

Practice C

Work with a partner. How many similar facts about your country can you think of? Now compare your sentences with the rest of the class.

Practice D

What do these symbols tell you you *must not* do?

Practice E

What rules does your institution have? Make a list using *must* and *must not*.

Reading

Read Mrs Jackson's letter and transfer the information to the holiday option form.

> 3 Carlton Avenue,
> London NW5 1RD.
> 071 699 3321
>
> Sunhols,
> 26 Queen Street,
> London W2P 5AG.
>
>
> 3 March 1991
>
>
> Dear Sir,
>   I wish to book holiday number TL159 from the Sunhols brochure. There are four of us travelling: my husband and I, and our two children aged 14 and 17.
>   We would like to leave from Gatwick Airport on Saturday, 19 July and return from Dalaman on Saturday, 2 August. The resort we have chosen is Kalkan.
>   We would like two twin-bedded rooms with bathroom in the Marmaris Hotel.
>   Please telephone if you require any further information.
>
>   Yours faithfully,
>
>   *R Jackson*
>
>   Rita Jackson

Writing

Mrs Jackson receives a telephone call from Sunhols saying that the holiday is available and asking for a deposit to secure the option. When Sunhols receive the deposit, they write a letter of confirmation to Mrs Jackson.

Finish the letter from Sunhols.

1 Confirm the details of the holiday.
2 Ask for payment of the balance eight weeks before departure.

>
>
> **SUNHOLS**
>
> 26, Queen Street, London W2P 5AG
> Tel: 071-275 6342
>
> FAX 071-275 6785
> Telex 97835S
>
> **our reference** JA/PMS
>
> Mrs R Jackson
> 3 Carlton Avenue
> London NW5 1RD
>
>
> 15 March 1991
>
>
> Dear Mrs Jackson
>
> Thank you for your letter of 3 March.
>
> We would like to confirm the booking of your holiday ...

HOLIDAY OPTION FORM

Client's Name ....

Address ....

....

....

....

Phone ....

DETAILS

Tour Operator
Destination
Hotel
Accommodation
Departure Airport
Date
Duration
Holiday No.

Activity

Look at the information on the holiday in Japan.

Tariff: £740
Single supplement: £150

Departure schedule:

Daily from Hong Kong, except New Year –
28 December to 03 January.

Important Notes:

1) Hotels: The new Miyako or similar in
Kyoto, the Grand Palace in Tokyo.
2) US passport holders will require visas
for Japan.
3) One excursion each in Kyoto and Tokyo
is included in the tour cost.

**For all arrangements the inclusions are as
follows:**

– Twin sharing accommodation at hotels
indicated in each programme (or hotels of
similar standard).
– flights from Hong Kong and to Europe.
– transfers.
– services of local English-speaking agents.

Not included:

Meals, excursions, gratuities, visas (if
applicable), airport taxes, insurance,
incidental expenditure.

Now look again at the dialogue on page 28. Make a
similar dialogue between a travel agent and a
customer.

Useful expressions:

☐ *I'm interested in . . .*
☐ *The price includes . . .*
☐ *There's a single-room supplement/deposit of . . .*

Summary

Now you can

- Explain about travel arrangements and conditions
  The balance is due . . .
  I can keep an option open on the holiday.

- Talk and ask about obligation
  After that you must confirm.
  You needn't confirm straight away.
  Do I have to pay extra for a single room?

- Write letters of confirmation

New words

accommodation	internal
allowed	invoice
amount	licence
apply	option
balance	prohibition
client	provisional
duration	requirement
excursion	resort
FAX	transfer
gratuity	twin-bedded
insurance	visa

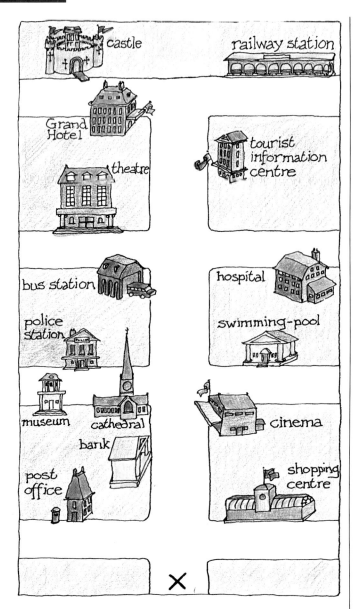

Reading

Look at the street map. Imagine you are standing at the point marked with a cross. Where do these directions take you?

1 Go straight down this road, take the second turning on the left, and it's on the right.
2 Go along this road, take the third turning on the right, and it's on the right.
3 Keep straight on until you get to the end of the road, then turn left, and it's on the right.
4 Go down as far as the cinema, then turn right, and it's on the left.
5 Keep straight on past the cathedral, then turn left at the bus station, and it's on the right.

Language study

| Go | straight | down along | this road | as far as past to | the bank. |

| Take the | first second third | turning | on the | right. left |

| Turn | left right | at after | the bus station. |

Practice A

Now give similar directions to these destinations:

1 the shopping centre
2 the Tourist Information Centre
3 the railway station
4 the post office
5 the Grand Hotel

Practice B

You are at the Tourist Information Centre. Working in pairs, use the map to ask each other the way to:

the post office
the castle
the bank
the museum
the Grand Hotel
the railway station
the swimming-pool

Example: **A** *Excuse me. Can you tell me how to get to the post office, please?*
B *Certainly. Turn left, then take the third turning on the right.*

Practice C

Work in pairs. Choose another point on the map to start from. Now choose three destinations and ask your partner how to get to them. Take turns.

Listening

Listen to the description of the airport terminal. Can you name the places 1–6 on the plan?

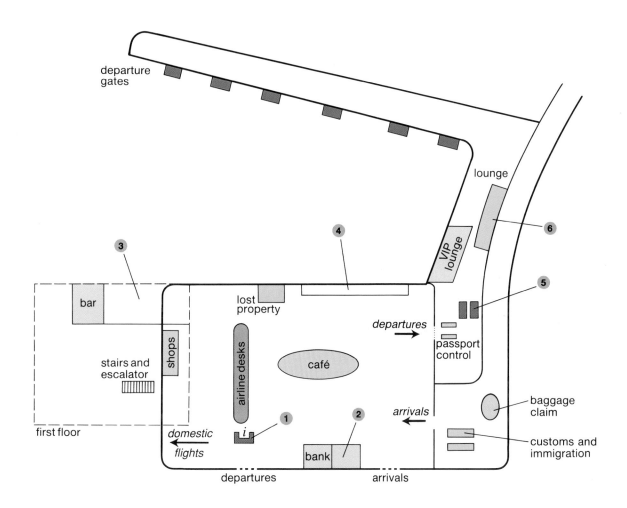

Practice D

You are on duty at the Information Desk. Help these travellers find what they want:

1   Where can I buy a newspaper?
2   Where's the lost property office, please?
3   I need to change some money.
4   Is there a car hire office here?
5   Is there a bar?
6   I want to buy a ticket.
7   Where's the duty-free shop?
8   Do domestic flights leave from this terminal?

Reading

Before you look at the text, try to answer these questions.

1 How many Tourist Information Centres (TICs) do you think there are in Britain?
2 Do you think they close at weekends?
3 Do you think it is expensive to book accommodation at a TIC?
4 Do you think you can book accommodation in advance if you write to a TIC?

Now read the text and find out if you were right.

TOURIST INFORMATION CENTRES

There are over 700 Tourist Information Centres (TICs) in Britain.

You will usually find TICs centrally positioned in towns or beside main roads, and at points of entry into Britain – look out for this sign:

In London there are the British Travel Centre and Tourist Information Centres which specialize in England, Scotland, Wales and Northern Ireland.

Most TICs are open Monday to Friday, 09.00 to 17.00, although in summer many are open longer and at weekends. Some are open from Easter to September only.

Accommodation booking

Wherever you go, TICs will help you find accommodation for the night. Many centres will make a reservation for the same night in their locality – in England a small charge is usually made (about 95p); in Scotland the service is free (a small deposit is refunded at the end of the stay); in Wales and Northern Ireland the service is free. A number of them also offer a reservation service enabling you to arrange accommodation for the same or the next night in a different locality (providing the service also operates there). This linked accommodation service is known as Book-a-Bed-Ahead.

Please note that the centres do not make advance bookings by mail or telephone. You are advised to call in personally at the TIC and book your night's accommodation before 16.00.

Look at the map and pictures. Which places would you like to visit? Discuss the reasons for your choices.

York

Oxford

London

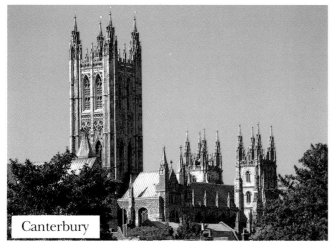

Canterbury

Brighton

Activity

Work in pairs. Draw a plan of the building you are in or a building you both know well. Take turns to ask each other directions around it.

Example: **A** *Excuse me? Can you tell me how to get to the toilets, please?*

B *Turn right, take the stairs to the first floor, then turn left, and they're at the end of the corridor.*

Summary

Now you can

- Direct people around streets and buildings
  Go down this street and take the third turning on the left.
  Take the stairs to the first floor, then turn right.

- Talk about airport services and facilities
  The restaurant is upstairs.
  The duty-free shop is on the right of the departure lounge.

- Talk about Tourist Information Centres in Britain

New words

advance	escalator
booking	facilities
airport security	first floor
boarding card	give directions
building	goods
car hire office	locality
corridor	lost property office
departure lounge	passport control
direct	stairs
domestic	street map
duty-free shop	tax-free
Easter	terminal

Listening

Lucy Tan works in a busy tourist information office in the centre of Singapore. Listen to this dialogue and tick the places she mentions.

Little India   ☐
Chinatown   ☐
The Chinese Garden   ☐
The Botanic Gardens   ☐
Arab Street   ☐
Raffles Hotel   ☐
Newton Circus   ☐
Jurong Bird Park   ☐

Language study

Advice

*You **ought to*** | *contact the police.*
*You **should***

Suggestions

*You **could** (always)* | *take a bus.*
*I **suggest** you*

Practice A

Match these sentences.

1   I can't find my passport.
2   My wife is feeling very ill.
3   How do I get to the airport?
4   Where can I change money on a Sunday?
5   Are there any good French restaurants?
6   I'm only in London for the day.
7   I've lost my ticket.

a   You ought to contact the airline.
b   You could try La Belle Angele.
c   I suggest you try your hotel.
d   You ought to contact the police.
e   Then you should visit Buckingham Palace.
f   You could always take a bus.
g   You should take her to hospital.

Practice B

Work with a partner. Take turns to be a tourist and a tourist information officer in a city you know. Ask for and make suggestions.

Example: London
      A   *What do you suggest I do on Monday morning?*
      B   *You could visit Buckingham Palace.*

Choose a different day and time for each suggestion.

Practice C

Make short dialogues using these prompts. Take turns to give advice and make suggestions.

1   You're not sure where to go on holiday.
2   You want to know a good film to see.
3   You're not happy with your job.
4   You don't know what to do next weekend.

Reading

Work in pairs. **Student A** reads the passage about Hong Kong and **Student B** reads the passage about Acapulco. Read *one* passage only. You must tell your partner about your passage, without looking at it. You may take short notes, but you must not write down more than *twenty* words.

Hong Kong offers you...

Hong Kong has a great range of tours, all of which can be booked through our local representative on arrival.

Travel around Hong Kong Island. See the wonderful view from Victoria Peak or explore the world-famous Stanley Market from a junk. Take a tram along the waterfront and walk round the old Hong Kong.

Watch dolphins perform in the largest oceanarium in Asia or, for those interested in history, there's Sung Dynasty village – a replica village of China 1000 years ago.

If you are interested in sports, Hong Kong has plenty to offer: golf, squash, and windsurfing, as well as facilities for playing tennis, rugby, bowls, and cricket. Or why not visit Hong Kong races at Happy Valley and Shatin racecourses?

You could, of course, just relax on the sandy beaches of Lantau Island with its tea plantations, fishing villages, and green mountains, or visit the Buddhist monastery of Po Lin.

ACAPULCO

Acapulco is Mexico's most glamorous resort, where the sun shines 300 days a year, and where the nightlife enjoys an international reputation.

By day, take a cruise on a catamaran round the Bahía de Acapulco, one of the world's most beautiful bays, or sit in the shade of a palm tree or under a *palapa* on one of the many splendid beaches.

Those who are more energetic can stroll around Old Acapulco, with its famous bullring, Plaza Caletilla, and watch the *clavadistas* leaping 40 metres into the sea from the cliff at La Quebrada.

By night, dine on fresh seafood at a romantic rooftop restaurant, then dance until dawn in one of the many discos in 'The Strip'. Alternatively, you could relax in a nightclub, or go on a late-night shopping trip for clothing, jewellery, and handicrafts.

palapa = a straw parasol

clavadista = cliff-diver

Writing

Now it is your turn to write about the tourist attractions of a city. You may find some useful ideas in the passages. Choose one of the tasks below.

1 Look at these pictures and notes about these places in and around London and write a short description of them.

Colourful capital: sights, shopping, nightlife.

Sights
Boat-trip – see Tower Bridge, the Tower of London, the Houses of Parliament.
Bus-trip – see Trafalgar Square, Piccadilly Circus, Buckingham Palace, St Paul's Cathedral.

Shopping
Oxford Street – clothes, jewellery.
Covent Garden – unusual shops, restaurants, cafés.

Nightlife
West End theatres – the latest plays and shows.
The Royal Festival Hall or *Barbican Hall* – classical concerts.
The Hippodrome or *Stringfellows* – discotheques.
Wide range of restaurants – international cuisine.

2 Write a description of a town or city that you know well.

Activity

Work in pairs. Choose a city that you know about, or one of the cities from this unit, and make a dialogue between a tourist information officer and a visitor to the city.

Tourist Information Officer
Make a list of the things to do and see in the city and give advice and suggestions to the tourist.

Tourist
Find out what there is to see and do in the city. Explain that you are only visiting for a short time and ask for some advice and suggestions.

Summary

Now you can

- ☐ Talk about city highlights
  Singapore is full of restaurants.
  Acapulco is Mexico's most glamorous resort.

- ☐ Offer suggestions and advice
  You should try to visit Raffles Hotel.
  You could take a bus tour.

- ☐ Write about the attractions of resorts and cities

New words

bay	nightlife
beach	oceanarium
bullring	open-air
catamaran	peak
cliff	racecourse
cruise	reputation
explore	squash
handicraft	stall
jewellery	stroll
junk	tram
monastery	waterfront

Listening 1

Before you read the text, listen to this story.

Did you find it difficult to believe? Now read the story and fill the gaps with the past tense of the following verbs:

go/check/have/interview/feel/burn/find/be (×2)/start/come to

In 1990 a visitor to the USA . . . into a hotel in New York. He . . . to his room, but . . . cold because the air-conditioning . . . on, so he took the curtains, the sheets, and the towels and . . . a fire in the middle of the floor. The entire hotel . . . down. Luckily there . . . no casualties. His bill for one night (without breakfast) . . . over $65,000,000. When the police . . . him the following day, they . . . that he . . . a total of $16. The daily rate for his room was $120.

Language study

We form questions and negatives in the past using *did* and the infinitive.

*Where **did** he **start** the fire?*
*He **didn't have** enough money.*

Notice that the past tense of the verb 'be' is *was/were* (even for questions and negatives).

*The man **was** a visitor to New York.*
*Why **was** he cold?*
*There **weren't** any casualties.*

Practice A

The regular *-ed* ending can be pronounced in three different ways. Can you match these verbs with the correct sound?

started	worked	watched	sailed	turned
lived	landed	pulled	seemed	ended
painted	booked	counted	asked	missed

/-t/	/-d/	/-ıd/
*wash**ed***	*serv**ed***	*want**ed***
. . .	. . .	. . .

Practice B

Can you complete the past forms of these common verbs?

Example: swim – *swam*

1 fall
2 make
3 see
4 speak
5 catch
6 break
7 buy
8 bring
9 pay
10 travel
11 fly
12 spend

Practice C

Make questions about the text in **Listening 1** using the prompts.

Example: Why/he/start/fire?
           Why did he start the fire?

1 Where/he/come from?
2 Where/be/hotel?
3 What/he/use/start/fire?
4 What/happen/hotel?
5 How much/be/man's bill?
6 Who/interview/him/following day?
7 How much money/man/have?
8 What/be/daily rate/his room?

Practice D

Find out about your partner. Take turns to ask and answer questions about last year. Use the prompts below. If your partner answers *Yes*, try to find out more.

move house/change your hair-style/buy a car/fall in love/go abroad on holiday/meet someone special/take an exam

Example: **A** *Did you go abroad on holiday last year?*
           B *Yes, I did.*
           A *Where did you go?*
           B *I went to England.*

LET'S HOPE THE WEATHER IN ENGLAND IS BETTER THIS YEAR

Listening 2

Listen to the three dialogues and complete the details on the invoice, the transaction slip, and the hotel bill.

Dialogue 1

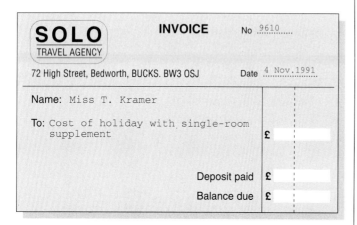

SOLO TRAVEL AGENCY

INVOICE   No 9610

72 High Street, Bedworth, BUCKS. BW3 OSJ   Date 4 Nov.1991

Name: Miss T. Kramer

To: Cost of holiday with single-room supplement   £

Deposit paid   £

Balance due   £

Dialogue 2

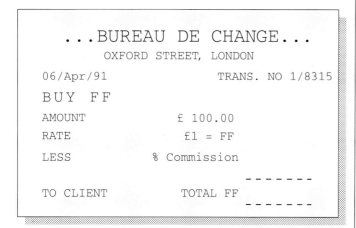

...BUREAU DE CHANGE...
OXFORD STREET, LONDON

06/Apr/91   TRANS. NO 1/8315

BUY FF

AMOUNT   £ 100.00
RATE   £1 = FF
LESS   % Commission
                  _ _ _ _ _ _
TO CLIENT   TOTAL FF
                  _ _ _ _ _ _

Dialogue 3

HOTEL CARLO
VIALE MICHELANGELO 172
50125 FIRENZE

Sig. / Name : Blair   Appart. / Room :

	Data/ Date	Causale/ Description	Importo/ Amount
Prezzo comprensivo di servizio e tasse *Service and taxes included in price*	22.10	App/Room	L 120,000

Mezzo di pagamento/ *Method of payment*		Totale/ *Total* L.

Reading

More and more people are using credit cards to pay for tickets, holidays, etc. Do you know the procedures for accepting credit card payments?

Imagine you work in a travel agency. What would you do in the following situations?

1   A man wants to pay for a holiday by credit card. You notice that the card has no signature.
2   A woman tries to use her credit card to pay for some tickets. You notice that the card expired the previous day.
3   Someone wishes to make a credit card payment by telephone.

Discuss your answers with a partner. Then read the procedures below to see if you were right.

MEMORANDUM   **TIKITRAVEL**

To All Staff   **Date** 18 August 1991
From General Manager   **Ref**
Subject Accepting credit card payments

1   Always ensure that the credit card is valid. The expiry date appears on the card. Note that some cards also carry a 'Not valid before' date. If the card is invalid, you must obtain authorization from the appropriate credit card company.

2   The card holder's signature must appear on the card. Holders of unsigned cards must produce proof of identity and signature, then sign the card in front of a staff member.

3   Check that the credit card is not on the blacklist of the issuing company.

4   The amount to be charged must not exceed the limit set by the credit card company. For amounts above the limit, authorization is necessary.

5   Cards that are damaged or defaced in any way are invalid.

6   In the case of telephone sales, make sure you note the following details:

    - name of card holder
    - credit card type
    - card number
    - expiry date
    - address of card holder (to which credit card statement is usually sent)
    - contact telephone number

Activity

Work in pairs. Take turns to be the tourist and the travel agent.

Tourist

Make a telephone booking of your 26-day holiday to the Himalayas and the Tibetan Plateau. Say you want a single room. Ask for insurance cover. Ask for the total cost. Say you want to pay by credit card. Remember that the travel agent will ask you for details.

Travel agent

Here are the details of the holiday that the tourist wants to book by telephone.

The Mountain Peoples of the Himalayas and the Tibetan Plateau
(Tour code: MONI/2)

Departure Schedule	Tariff
05 May	£3600.00
22 September	£3600.00

Deposit: £300.00

Single Room Supplement: £795.00

You can offer comprehensive travel insurance for £47.20 extra. Calculate the total cost of the holiday. Ask for an immediate deposit. Tell the tourist what the balance is. Ask for credit card details.

Writing

Write your diary for yesterday.

Example: *I woke up at . . .*

Summary

Now you can

- Deal with payments
  Including the single-room supplement, that comes to £645.
  We charge 2% commission on each transaction.
  How would you like to pay?

- Use the past tense of regular and irregular verbs
  Did you go abroad on holiday last year?
  Yes, I went to Scotland.

New words

authorization	invalid
bill	limit
blacklist	payment
calculate	printout
card holder	procedure
cashier	receipt
commission	reception
comprehensive	signature
currency	supplement
exchange rate	tariff
expire	transaction
identity	valid

Reading

Which hotel:

	Alexander	Apollo	Helena
1 is the biggest?	☐	☑	☐
2 is nearest the beach?	☐	☐	☐
3 is the most luxurious?	☐	☐	☐
4 has the best facilities?	☐	☐	☐
5 has the widest choice of restaurants?	☐	☐	☐
6 is the cheapest?	☐	☐	☐

True or false?

7 The Helena is more expensive than the Apollo.

8 The Apollo is farther from the beach than the Alexander.

9 The Alexander has the largest number of rooms.

10 The Alexander has more tennis courts than squash courts.

Alexander Hotel ★★★★★

420 rooms

2 restaurants, bar, 2 pools, 6 tennis courts, 2 squash courts, jacuzzi

10 minutes' walk from beach

£380 (for 7 nights)

Helena Hotel ★★★

320 rooms

restaurant, bar, tennis court

15 minutes' walk from beach

£290 (for 7 nights)

Apollo Hotel ★★★★

540 rooms

restaurant, pool, 2 tennis courts, shop

5 minutes' walk from beach

£310 (for 7 nights)

Language study

1 Most adjectives of one syllable (e.g. cheap, near, small) end *-er* in the comparative and *-est* in the superlative.

*quick   quicker   **the** quick**est***

2 Adjectives of three syllables or more (e.g. beautiful, expensive) take *more* in the comparative and *the most* in the superlative.

*expensive   **more** expensive   **the most** expensive*

3 Two-syllable adjectives ending in *-y* follow rule 1.

*happy   happi**er**   **the** happi**est*** (notice the spelling change)

Other two-syllable adjectives sometimes follow rule 1 and sometimes follow rule 2.

*quiet   quiet**er**   **the** quiet**est***
*modern   **more** modern   **the most** modern*

4 After comparatives (e.g. *happier*/*more modern*) we use *than*.

5 Here are some common adjectives with irregular formations:

	Comparative	*Superlative*
good	better	the best
bad	worse	the worst
far	farther	the farthest

Practice A

Complete these sentences using *the most* . . . or *the -est*.

1 I think Chinese is . . . language to speak in the world. (difficult)
2 Alan is . . . person I know. (lazy)
3 Your hotel is . . . from the beach. (far)
4 This country has . . . weather in the world. (bad)
5 This is . . . part of the river. (wide)
6 It's . . . hotel in the city. (modern)
7 She is . . . girl in the school. (pretty)
8 . . . city in Scotland is Glasgow. (large)

Practice B

Complete these sentences using the comparative or superlative form of the word in brackets. You may need to use more than one word.

1 Air travel is . . . rail travel. (quick)
2 Travelling by taxi is . . . travelling by bus. (expensive)
3 Tokyo is . . . Rome. (big)
4 Everest is . . . mountain in the world. (high)
5 The Pacific Ocean is . . . the Atlantic. (large)
6 Egypt has much . . . summers than the UK. (hot)
7 The Amazon and the Nile are the two . . . rivers in the world. (long)
8 Adventure holidays are . . . beach holidays. (exciting)

Practice C

Read the passages about the Oriental Hotel in Bangkok and the Argao Beach Club Hotel in the Philippines.

Now compare the following features of the two hotels. Use the adjectives in brackets to help you.

watersports (*good for*)/room facilities (*luxurious*)/ choice of restaurant (*wide*)/location (*peaceful*)/ shopping (*convenient for*)/price (*cheap* or *expensive*)

Example: beach (*near*)
The Argao Beach Club Hotel is nearer the beach than the Oriental.

The Oriental in Bangkok is consistently named as one of the top three hotels in the world. Its 394 rooms are spacious and tastefully decorated. All have private bathroom, air-conditioning, hair-drier, TV with in-house movies, and mini-bar. Guests have a choice of seven restaurants including the 'Normandie Grill' for French cuisine, the 'Lord Jim' for seafood, and the 'Sala Rim Nam', which serves exotic Thai cuisine.

The hotel has two swimming-pools, and across the river is the Oriental's fully-equipped sports complex which offers tennis and squash facilities, a gymnasium, a sauna, a jogging track, and a fitness centre. There is entertainment most evenings, including a regular disco.

The informal **Argao Beach Club Hotel** is the perfect place for a 'get-away-from-it-all' holiday. It is hidden in a coconut grove on the beautiful Dalguete coastline in the Philippines. The white coral beach stretches for 2 km and the hotel's three coves have crystal-clear waters, rich in tropical marine life.

The hotel restaurant overlooks the sea and offers both native seafood specialities and a high standard of international cuisine. The hotel's 135 bedrooms are simply furnished with separate shower and wc, air-conditioning, and patio. A full range of watersports is available. There are also tennis courts, a games room, a sauna, and a jacuzzi. There is local entertainment with occasional floor shows, and a disco.

Listening

Look at the map and write down the clues you hear on the cassette. Which country is the man describing? Now make similar clues for other countries and test your partner.

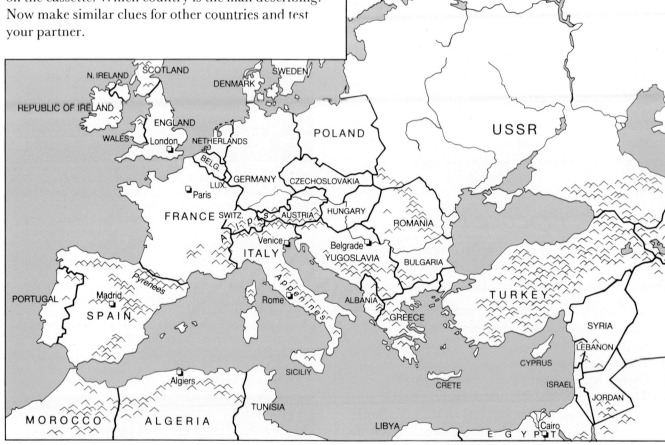

Activity

Work in pairs or small groups. Imagine you are going to build the ideal hotel. Where will it be? How big will it be? What facilities will it have? What will it be called? Makes notes (and drawings, if you like), then present your hotel to the rest of the class. Which hotel would you most like to stay at?

Writing

Look at these pictures and write a description of the hotel and its facilities. Use the information about the Oriental and the Argao Beach Club Hotels to help you.

Summary

Now you can

- Describe hotel facilities
  *All rooms have air-conditioning and a mini-bar.
  The Oriental is one of the most luxurious hotels in the world.*

- Make comparisons
  *The Alexander has better facilities than the Apollo.
  Yugoslavia is bigger than Portugal but smaller than France.*

New words

coastline	location
coral	marine life
cove	mini-bar
cuisine	native
entertainment	overlook
fitness centre	patio
gymnasium	sauna
informal	seafood
jacuzzi	sports complex

Listening

Lotus Tours are thinking of including the Golden
Sands Hotel in their list of Turkish hotels. Listen to
the Lotus representative talking to the hotel's General
Manager. Write *n* next to the features which the hotel
has *now*, and *p* next to the features which are *planned*:

twins/doubles with balcony and beach view	...
twins/doubles with garden view	...
deluxe doubles	...
family rooms	...
interconnecting rooms	...
restaurant	...
poolside bar	...
use of watersports club facilities	...
swimming-pool	...

Language study

We use *be* + *going to* to talk about plans and
intentions:

We're going to start building an extension.

and to talk about something that we can see is likely
to happen:

*I think it's **going to** rain.*(There are grey clouds in the
sky.)

Practice A

Make questions with *going to* using the prompts below.

Example: I must get to London today! (How/get there?)
How are you going to get there?

1 I've got to find a telephone. (Who/call?)
2 I'm spending next week in Paris. (Where/stay?)
3 I'm going to the cinema tonight. (What/see?)
4 I'm going shopping. (What/buy?)
5 Paul's thinking of getting married. (Who/marry?)

Practice B

Look at these pictures. What is going to happen?

Practice C

What plans have you got for: this evening?
next weekend?
next year?

Make notes. Then, in pairs, take turns to ask and answer questions.

Example: **A** *What are you going to do this evening?*
B *Well, first I'm going to have a bath. Then . . .*

Reading

Read the following advertisement on weekend breaks. Some words have been left out. Fill in the gaps with the words below. Use each word once.

every/especially/picturesque/reduced/leisure/
international/private/colour/elegant/historic

A weekend break...

Choose from over 50 hotels in . . . towns and . . . countryside.

Families are . . . welcome – most children stay at a . . . rate and some even stay **FREE**.

Each bedroom has a . . . bathroom, . . . TV, radio, telephone, and hair-drier. In . . . bedroom you will find a courtesy tray with facilities for making tea and coffee.

Many hotels have . . . centres with sauna, mini-bar, gymnasium, jacuzzi, and solarium, along with a light refreshment lounge. They may also offer golf, tennis, swimming, and much more.

Of course every hotel has a superb bar and restaurant facilities – . . . dining-rooms and . . . cuisine.

For more information, write to:

Activity

The three families below are going to Amsterdam on a weekend break.

1   Mr and Mrs Mills: a young couple on their honeymoon. They would like somewhere quiet and romantic, with a good restaurant. They would prefer a room with a bathroom rather than a shower.

2   Mr and Mrs Gordon-Brown: an elderly couple who want somewhere as central and as cheap as possible.

3   Mr and Mrs Henderson: a couple in their mid-thirties, with a son aged 11 and a daughter aged 12. They have friends in Amsterdam so they won't often be eating in the hotel. Mr Henderson likes to go jogging in the morning. Their children want a hotel where there will be other young people.

Work in pairs. Study the information about the hotels below. Which hotel would you advise each family to stay at?

Bergman ★★★

A small hotel of only 16 rooms. Situated in a quiet, residential area behind Vondel Park, it overlooks a small canal and the park itself. The bedrooms have their own shower, TV, and radio. Twin rooms with bath are available at a supplement. Although the hotel does not have a restaurant or bar, the dining room is very pleasant and drinks are served on request.

We recommend early booking because of the limited accommodation available.

NO ROOM CHARGE for 1 child under 12 sharing room with 2 adults. (Meals payable direct).

Supplements per person per night:
Twin with Bath   £4.00
Single with Shower   £8.00

ONE NIGHT FREE in stays of 3 nights or more
1 Jan - 26 Feb, 1 - 27 Jun & 15 Nov - 28 Dec

Embassy ★★ superior

Once a private house with a rich history, this hotel is highly recommended for the standard of its accommodation.

Because of the nature of the building all rooms are different, each with its own character, and they are on a number of levels. There are larger, superior rooms with a view of the canal (available at a supplement).

Downstairs you will find a quiet little bar and a small breakfast room. The hotel has no lift and some of the stairs are quite steep so please request a downstairs room if the stairs could be a problem. All rooms have private shower.

Supplements per person per night:
Superior Twin with Canal View   £7.00
Single Room   £11.00

ONE NIGHT FREE in stays of 4 nights or more
1 Jan - 15 Mar & 1 Nov - 31 Dec

Empire ★★★★ luxe

An international deluxe hotel in one of Amsterdam's most fashionable areas. The Empire has 250 guest rooms and suites which either overlook the canal or the gracious tree-lined Apollolaan. All the bedrooms have telephone, minibar, colour TV and hairdrier.

The hotel has 2 restaurants, 'The Veranda', which serves international cuisine, and 'The Santori', an elegant Japanese restaurant. The bar overlooking the canal, a discotheque, and casino complete this wonderful hotel.

NO ROOM CHARGE for 1 child under 12 sharing room with 2 adults. (Meals payable direct).

Single Room Supplement   £24.00 per night.

Writing

After his visit to the Golden Sands Hotel, the Lotus representative decided to recommend to Head Office that they should negotiate an agreement with the hotel.

Listen to the dialogue again and note down as many details as possible about the hotel. Remember that you already have some of the information on page 48. Then write the representative's letter.

Start the letter like this:

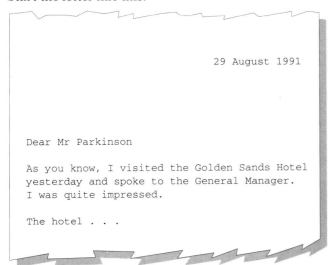

29 August 1991

Dear Mr Parkinson

As you know, I visited the Golden Sands Hotel yesterday and spoke to the General Manager. I was quite impressed.

The hotel . . .

Finish the letter like this:

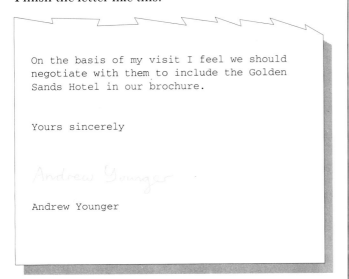

On the basis of my visit I feel we should negotiate with them to include the Golden Sands Hotel in our brochure.

Yours sincerely

Andrew Younger

Andrew Younger

Summary

Now you can

▪ Talk about hotel room types and facilities
There are 120 rooms plus two suites, each with its own jacuzzi and private bar.
There are several interconnecting doubles on each floor.

▪ Talk about plans and intentions
At the end of this season we're going to start building an extension.
We're going to try to negotiate a deal with the watersports club.

▪ Write letters of recommendation

New words

advertisement	impressed
balcony	interconnecting
category	negotiate
couple	poolside
double	season
extension	solarium
family room	suite
hair-drier	watersports
honeymoon	weekend break

Listening

As you listen to the telephone conversation, complete the information on the screen below.

```
            MOUNTJOY HOTEL - NEWCASTLE

         ----- RESERVATION CONFIRMATION -----


    ENTRY DATE:      3 JULY 1991
    ACCOMMODATION:   NOT CONFIRMED
    RESERVATION FOR:
    CONTACT:         OLIVER ELECTRONICS, LONDON
    NO. OF PERSONS:
    ARRIVING:
    FOR:                          NIGHTS
    CHECK-IN TIME:
    ROOM TYPE:
    ROOM RATE:       £65.00
```

Language study 1

We use *will* to talk about things we expect to happen. We use *won't* to talk about things we don't expect to happen.

*Mr Williams **will** probably arrive quite late.*
*I **won't** see you tomorrow. I'm working at home.*

We also use *will* when we decide to do something at the moment we speak.

*One moment. **I'll** put you through.*
***I'll** just check that.*

Practice A

Complete the decisions below with *I'll* and a suitable verb.

Example: The train is late. I think . . . a taxi.
          The train is late. I think I'll take a taxi.

1 Phew! It's hot in here. I think . . . the window.
2 Can you confirm by fax?
   Yes . . . that immediately.
3 The telephone's ringing!
   . . . it!
4 I'm feeling tired. I don't think . . . out tonight.
5 What would you like to drink?
   . . . a mineral water, please.
6 John was late again today.
   OK. . . . to him later.
7 I think . . . abroad on holiday this year.
8 Have you still got my book?
   Yes. . . . it back to you tomorrow.

Practice B

Work in pairs. Take turns to decide what to do in these situations.

Example: You are feeling sick.
      A *I think I'll lie down.*
      B *I think I'll go to the doctor's.*

1   You are thirsty.
2   You can't sleep at night.
3   You want to take some exercise.
4   You don't like your job.
5   You are feeling tired.
6   You've found some money in the street.

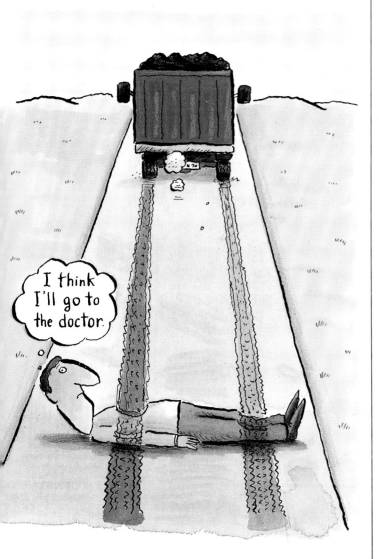

I think I'll go to the doctor.

Practice C

What do you expect to happen in the future? Tell your partner about yourself using *will* or *won't* and the prompts below.

get married/live to be 80 or older/be rich/be famous/ work abroad/pass my next exam

Examples: *I'll probably get married.*
             I won't be rich.

Language study 2

Time prepositions

*I'd like to book a room **for** four nights **from** 10 August.*
*She's getting married **in** April.*
*I'll be thirty **in** 1999.*
*He's coming **on** Tuesday/**on** 8 September.*
*We are open **at** 6 p.m./**at** Easter/**at** New Year.*
*Can you hold the room **until** 10.00 p.m.?* (for the period of time from now to 10.00 p.m.)
*Please confirm **by** Friday.* (not later than Friday)

Practice D

Fill the gaps in these sentences with a suitable preposition from **Language study 2**.

1   My exam is . . . 4 May.
2   My sister's birthday is . . . September.
3   You must pay the balance . . . 10 June.
4   The restaurant is open . . . 2 p.m. . . . . midnight.
5   The swimming-pool is always closed . . . Sunday(s).
6   I'm visiting my family . . . Christmas.
7   The ticket is valid . . . three months . . . 1 May.
8   It's valid . . . 31 July.
9   You must cancel . . . tomorrow at the latest, or you will lose your deposit.
10 They are staying . . . two weeks.
11 I was born . . . 1973.
12 I always go to bed . . . 11 p.m. exactly.

Practice E

Complete the FAX sent by Mr Williams's secretary to confirm his reservation.

```
SENT BY:Xerox Telecopier 7021
4-7-91;12:18;OLIVER EL.*0865310423;#


Dear Sir,

Hotel booking for Mr Williams,
Oliver Electronics

I·wish to ... the reservation of a
... room ... four nights ...
10.8.91 in the name of Williams.

Mr Williams ... probably arrive
late ... the evening. Please ...
the room ... 10.00pm.

Yours ...

Bella Richards
```

Telephone phrases

Look at how this hotel receptionist replies to different callers.

1 Hold the line, please. I'll put you through to reservations.
2 I'm afraid she isn't here at the moment. Can I take a message?
3 Would you like to speak to the Duty Manager?
4 Can I ask him to call you back?
5 I'm sorry. There's no answer from room 301.
6 Could you repeat that, please?
7 Just a moment. I'll check for you.
8 Could I have your name, please?
9 The line's busy at the moment. Will you hold?
10 If you give me your number, I'll call you back.

What do you think each caller said first?

Example: 1 *Hello. I'd like to reserve a room, please.*

Now listen to and repeat the phrases on the cassette. Check your pronunciation and intonation.

Reading

Look at these company guide-lines for using the telephone. Do you agree with all of them? Discuss your views with your partner, then with the rest of the class.

Guide to Telephone Behaviour

☎ Stand up before you answer the telephone. This will heighten your sense of authority.
☎ Answer the telephone promptly, within three rings if possible.
☎ Listen with your right ear on business calls. Your right ear is connected to the left (logical) side of the brain.
☎ Start each call by stating your name and position.
☎ Find out the caller's name and use it in the conversation.
☎ Listen. Try not to interrupt.
☎ Concentrate. Don't attempt to do two things at the same time.
☎ When the caller is speaking, make 'continuity noises' to let him/her know you are listening.
☎ Make notes and read them back to the caller to check you have got the correct message.
☎ If an incoming call is inconvenient, explain why, take the caller's name and number, and offer to call him/her back.
☎ Always smile into the mouthpiece. It shows in your voice.

Activity 1

If possible, sit back to back with a partner. Take turns to play both roles. Try to use some of the telephone phrases from the list above.

Receptionist

You work at the Holiday Palace Hotel. Study the extract from the hotel brochure. Help the caller with his/her enquiry. Make sure you find out the name and address, the dates they want, and the number of people. Ask him/her to confirm in writing.

This luxury hotel has exceptional facilities for leisure, sport and entertainment. The superb new Leisure Club has a heated swimming-pool, squash courts, sauna, sunbeds, jacuzzi, fully-equipped gym and 3 tennis courts.

All 178 bedrooms have a private bathroom and are luxuriously furnished and fitted with colour TV, in-house video, radio, direct dial telephone, hair-drier and tea/coffee-making facilities.

The hotel's 2 restaurants and 3 bars offer guests a real choice of wining and dining.

Guest

Your name is Mr/Mrs Kiel. Telephone the Holiday Palace Hotel to enquire about a week's holiday in June for yourself, your husband/wife and one child. Ask about the hotel's facilities. Give exact dates and agree to confirm in writing.

Activity 2

Now take turns to act out these roles.

Travel clerk

You work for Concord Travel. Mr Meyer, your manager, is out of the office this morning. You receive a telephone call for him. Ask for the caller's name. Offer to take a message for Mr Meyer.

Caller

Your name is Mr/Mrs Dyson. Telephone Concord Travel and ask to speak to the manager, Mr/Mrs Meyer. If the manager is not there, leave a message asking him/her to call you back this afternoon. You are in London. Your number is 071-458 2871.

Writing

Now write:

1 Mr/Mrs Kiel's letter of confirmation.
2 the telephone message for Mr Meyer.

Summary

Now you can

▪ Take room reservations
I'll just check that . . .
That's a single room for four nights from 10 August.

▪ Deal with telephone enquiries
I'm afraid she isn't here at the moment. Can I take a message?
The line's busy at the moment. Will you hold?

New words

authority	incoming
caller	inconvenient
closed	interrupt
confirmation	intonation
guide-lines	mouthpiece
heighten	pronunciation

Listening

Listen to the receptionist checking in a newly-arrived guest and complete the keycard.

HOTEL EXCELSIOR

KARL GUSTAVSGARTEN 7 · STOCKHOLM

Name ....

Room Number ....

Room Rate .... 700 Skr ....

Number of Nights ....

Departure Date ....

Language study

We use *if* to express possibility and *when* to show certainty. In the sentences below, *if* and *when* refer to future time, but they take the present simple tense.

*If you **want** something to eat, just call room service.*
*I'll ask him to call you **when** he **arrives**.*

Practice A

Fill the gaps in these sentences with *when* or *if*.

1 I'm going to a meeting now. I'll speak to you . . . I return.
2 I'll stay at home . . . it rains tomorrow.
3 Mrs Parry is coming here this morning. . . . she arrives, please show her into my office.
4 I will be surprised . . . we win the match.
5 . . . you don't like this room, I can show you another one.
6 . . . you are older, you will understand.

Practice B

Match the beginnings and ends of these sentences.

1 If you want to visit India,
2 If you wish to make an outside call,
3 When Mr Adams calls,
4 If you ask the receptionist,
5 If you want to pay with travellers' cheques,

a I will need to see some identification.
b she will arrange your alarm call.
c you will need a visa.
d can you give him a message?
e dial 9, followed by the number you want.

Practice C

Complete the sentences with *will*, *won't* or the present simple. All the sentences are about the future.

Example: If he . . . (want) to pass the exam, he . . . (have to) work hard.
           If he wants to pass the exam, he will have to work hard.

1 What do you want to do when you . . . (leave) school?
2 If she . . . (eat) that, she . . . (be) ill.
3 I . . . (cook) if you . . . (wash) the dishes.
4 When this programme . . . (end), I . . . go to bed.
5 If I . . . (see) John, I . . . (give) him your message.
6 Ask Peter to come and see me when he . . . (arrive).
7 If you . . . (not/leave) now, you . . . (not/catch) the train.
8 He . . . (do) it when he . . . (have) time.

Practice D

Ben works in a resort on a small island in the Seychelles. He is in a boat with a group of tourists on a fishing trip. The motor has stopped. The boat is about 1 km from the island, but it is moving slowly away. Ben is a good swimmer, but there are sharks in the water and it is getting dark. There is no fresh water. One of the women in the boat is feeling very ill.

What should Ben do? What will happen if Ben does nothing? Discuss possible answers using sentences starting *If* . . . How many sentences can you make?

Now write down four of your sentences.

Reading

Read the passage below. Some pairs of words are in italics. In each case, underline the word you think is correct. The first one has been done for you.

The hotel industry in Taiwan

Taiwan *currently/promptly* has *a total/an amount* of 104 tourist hotels. Taipei alone has 24 first class international hotels and dozens of tourist ones. The Tourism Bureau has established a hotel *rating/measuring* system called Plum Blossoms. Five Plum Blossoms *balances/equals* the standard international Five Star rating.

While most of Taiwan's top class hotels have standards similar to first-rate *establishments/enterprises* anywhere in the world, they also have a unique style of traditional Chinese service and *courtesy/kindness* that is difficult to find in the western world.

Chinese hotel *staff/members* approach service and *hospitality/welcome* as a highly refined art, not a tiresome *obligation/debt*. They really mean the saying of Confucius that 'When friends come from afar, is this not indeed a pleasure?'

Taiwan's most famous hotel is undoubtedly the Grand Hotel in Taipei. Situated on top of a ridge, it offers *excellent/valuable* views of the city. It is built in the classical imperial *style/method*, and its *ornate/deluxe* gardens and shaded paths give it a special air of peace and *dignity/pride* in contrast to the noise and bustle of the city below.

Writing

Here is the telex Mr Casado's secretary sent to reserve his room in Stockholm.

```
ATTN RESERVATIONS EXCELSIOR
HOTEL STOCKHOLM




PLS RESERVE ONE SGLB FOR TWO
NIGHTS FROM 20 DEC IN NAME OF
CASADO PLS CFM ASAP BY TLX
RGDS
```

See Appendix 3 for a list of common telex abbreviations.

1   Rewrite the telex above in plain language.

2   You work for Zap Travel, New York. Write a telex to the Swan Hotel, Stratford-upon-Avon, England, and reserve two double rooms and one single, all with bath, for five nights from 14 February, in the name of P. Noble. Ask for confirmation by telex as soon as possible.

3   Now write the telex reply to 2 above, confirming the booking.

Activity 1

Imagine that you have to promote your country's hotel industry to a group of tour operators from abroad. Work in pairs. Prepare notes on the features you will talk about (e.g. service, hospitality). Are there any famous hotels that you will mention?

Now present your talk to another pair, or to the rest of the class.

Activity 2

With a partner take turns to be a hotel receptionist and a business traveller.

Receptionist
You are the receptionist in a hotel in your town/city. The hotel has a restaurant and bar, but no room service. You are at the reception desk when a guest arrives. Help the guest to check in and tell him/her about the facilities.

Business traveller
You are on a business trip. You want to check into the hotel. You are expecting a telephone call from an important customer. What do you want the receptionist to do if the customer calls? Tell the receptionist that you want a late dinner in the hotel tonight, and that you want an alarm call in the morning.

Summary

Now you can

- Help arriving guests
  Would you like dinner tonight?
  Have a pleasant stay, sir.

- Use sentences with *when* and *if*
  Can you ask him to call me when he arrives?
  If you want something to eat later than that, just call room service.

- Read and write simple telexes

New words

alarm call	receptionist
bustle	refined
dial	shaded
establish	shark
identification	standard
imperial	traditional
pleasure	unique
rating	

'The customer is always right.' Do you agree with this statement? Discuss your views with a partner, then with the rest of the class.

Listening

1 Listen to the conversation between a travel agent and a customer.

a What is Sarah Ashton's complaint?
b How does the customer sound at the start of the conversation?
c How does she sound at the end of the conversation?
d Do you think the travel agent handled the complaint well? Say why.

2 Now listen to the conversation between a hotel receptionist and a guest.

a What two things does Mr Hagen complain about?
b Do you think he sounds angrier at the beginning of the conversation or at the end? Why?

3 Listen to the first conversation again. In pairs decide the best way of handling the customer's complaint. Compare your ideas with those of other students. Which solution do you like best?

Language study

Apologies

I'm (most) terribly sorry,
I'm so sorry,   *sir/madam.*
I do apologize,
Please accept my/our apologies,

Practice A

Work in pairs. Take turns to be the manager of a hotel and a guest. Use the prompts below to make short dialogues. Try to use a different expression to apologize each time.

no towels/no hot water/steak not cooked/TV not working/terrible coffee/noisy guest in next room/slow service/telephone not working

Example:

Guest: *I'd like to speak to the manager, please!*
Manager: *I'm the manager, madam. How can I be of assistance?*
Guest: *There are no towels in my room!*
Manager: *I'm so sorry, madam. I'll send some up straight away.*
Guest: *Thank you.*

"There are no towels in my bathroom."

Practice B

Sarah Ashton wrote a letter of complaint to the manager of the travel agency. Complete her letter with the correct tense of the verbs in brackets.

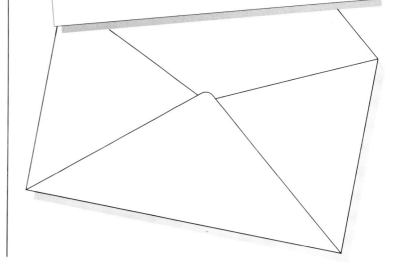

> 14 Cherry Street,
> Edinburgh EH12 1QT.
>
> 16th April 1991
>
> The Manager,
> Fly-By-Night Travel,
> 101 Constable Street,
> Edinburgh EH4 3PQ.
>
> Dear Sir,
>   I ... (write) to complain about the way a member of your staff ... (treat) me in Fly-By-Night Travel last Monday.
>   I ... (go) in to alter a flight booking to London (your ref. AST/3625/B) as a result of a mistake your office ... (make) in issuing my ticket.
>   I ... (try) to explain the situation to the travel clerk on duty, but he ... (be) extremely rude to me. He ... (suggest) that I was in the wrong and ... (tell) me that I would have to pay a supplement to upgrade my original ticket. In the end I ... (have to) pay an extra £50.
>   I often ... (fly) to London and always ... (use) Fly-By-Night, but if I ... (not/receive) a satisfactory reply to this letter, I ... (take) my business elsewhere.
>
>   Yours faithfully,
>
>   Sarah Ashton
>   Sarah Ashton

Reading and writing

First study the text below. Then look at the reply to Sarah Ashton's letter. Does it follow steps 1–4 in the passage? How can you improve it?

Replying to letters of complaint

It is important to deal quickly with letters of complaint. A prompt and satisfactory reply may save a customer.

First establish whether the complaint is justified. If you are quite sure the customer is at fault, your reply should politely point out what the facts are. If there is any doubt about responsibility for a mistake, it is often wiser to assume the customer is right.

Below is a guide to the content of a typical reply to a letter of complaint. Write about each point in a separate paragraph.

1 Begin your reply by acknowledging the fact that you have received the letter and referring to the complaint.

2 Then apologize for the mistake, explaining why it happened. Avoid blaming members of your staff.

3 Explain what action you are taking. This may mean replacing or repairing damaged goods, or refunding the customer's money.

4 Finally apologize for the inconvenience caused and indicate that you hope your business relationship can continue.

FLY-BY-NIGHT TRAVEL
101 Constable Street, Edinburgh EH4 3PQ
Tel: 031 333 9861   Fax: 031 333 9862

Sarah Ashton
14 Cherry Street
Edinburgh EH12 1QT

19 April 1991

Dear Ms Ashton

I do apologize for the inconvenience and hope you will decide to travel with us again.

I would like to apologize on behalf of the staff member who served you. He wishes you to know that he did not intend to cause you any offence.

Thank you for your letter of 16 April concerning your visit to Fly-By-Night Travel last Monday.

As a gesture of our goodwill I am enclosing a cheque for £50 to cover the supplement paid.

Yours sincerely

John Fleece

John Fleece
Manager

Now write a similar letter using the information below. Spend some time planning the letter before you start to write. You will have to invent some information.

You are the manager of a travel agency. You have received a letter of complaint from a Mr Webb. He asked your office to arrange his itinerary for a business trip to Brazil. The itinerary he received gave the wrong departure time. He missed his flight to São Paulo as well as a number of meetings.

Activity

Work in pairs. Choose one of the pictures above. What do you think the customer is complaining about? Use your imagination to make up a dialogue to suit the picture, then act out the scene with your partner.

Summary

Now you can

- Deal with complaints
  How can I be of assistance?
  I will ensure it doesn't happen again.

- Make apologies
  I'm terribly sorry, sir.
  I do apologize, madam.

- Reply to letters of complaint

New words

acknowledge	handle
apologies	inconvenience
cause offence	itinerary
complain	refund
complaint	relationship
document	satisfactory
gesture	supervisor
goodwill	upgrade

Listening

Greta Mueller is trying to arrange a conference for Tonini International. She is with the sales manager of the Plaza Hotel in Monte Carlo.

Look at Greta Mueller's checklist of requirements, then listen to her conversation. Tick the items that the hotel can provide.

Conference requirements

main room – theatre seating for 150
3 syndicate rooms
video recorder
back projection
photographer
secretarial help
interpreter
Autocue

Language study

We use *enough* and *too* with adjectives to show how big, beautiful, etc. things and people are.

adjective + *enough* | + *to* infinitive
too + adjective |

*Sue is rich **enough to** buy a Porsche.*
*These rooms are **too** small **to** hold 40 people.*

adjective + *enough* | + *for* + noun/pronoun
too + adjective |

*The ballroom is big **enough for** 200 people.*
*That shirt is **too** big **for** you.*

Notice that *not big enough = too small*
*These shoes aren't big **enough** = These shoes are **too** small.*

Practice A

Write the words in these sentences in the correct order.

1 small are for rooms the too conference these.
2 to is cold it swim too.
3 enough to is touch the he ceiling tall.
4 five big my enough people is for car not.
5 two steak is enough for this big people.
6 for easy this too is exercise me.

Practice B

Work in pairs. Make one sentence from each of the following pairs, using *too*.

Example: This food is extremely hot. I can't eat it.
           This food is too hot to eat.

1 It's dark. I can't see anything.
2 Bob is so small! He can't possibly join the army.
3 I'm very tired. I'm not going to the party tonight.
4 But you're so honest! I don't believe you're a politician!
5 I'm afraid Mr White is very busy. He can't see you today.
6 This suitcase is incredibly heavy. I can't carry it.

Practice C

Change the sentences below using *not . . . enough*.

Example: This room is too narrow.
           This room is not wide enough.

1 This coffee is too weak.
2 The water is too cold.
3 The bath is too small.
4 The ceiling is too low.
5 My bed is too short.
6 The service is too slow.

Practice D

Work in pairs. Imagine that you are interviewing people to work at reception in your hotel. Look at the advertisement:

RECEPTIONIST WANTED
to work in busy hotel. Aged 25-30. Smart appearance, outgoing personality, 12 months' experience in hotel work are essential. For further details contact:

Personnel Manager

The man below is interested in the job.

How many sentences can you make about the applicant, using *too . . ./not . . . enough*?

Example: *His hair is too long.*

Reading

Read the passage in which the Yorkshire and Humberside Tourist Board promote conferences in the region. Then summarize the extract by writing notes under the headings below.

YORKSHIRE HUMBERSIDE

WE'LL WELCOME YOU IN STYLE!

The location of your conference can play an important role in its success or failure.

The Yorkshire and Humberside region is an all-year-round location for conferences, business meetings, and seminars of any size and any duration. It is an area which can truly claim: 'It's all here!'.

The conference organizer can choose from a superb range of venues and accommodation, from peaceful country-house settings to large, but never impersonal, luxury hotels; from purpose-built conference centres with the most modern facilities and equipment, to highly individualized locations.

Wherever you go, you will find a warm Yorkshire welcome, a concern for the comfort of your delegates, and a personal commitment to ensuring the success of your conference.

Away from the conference floor, delegates and their partners can relax and enjoy the many attractions that Yorkshire and Humberside has to offer.

Serviced by a network of major motorways, a high-speed British Rail link, two airports and a major ferry port, it is easier than you think to bring your conference to Yorkshire and Humberside. A conference that really will be a 'BREATH OF FRESH AIR'.

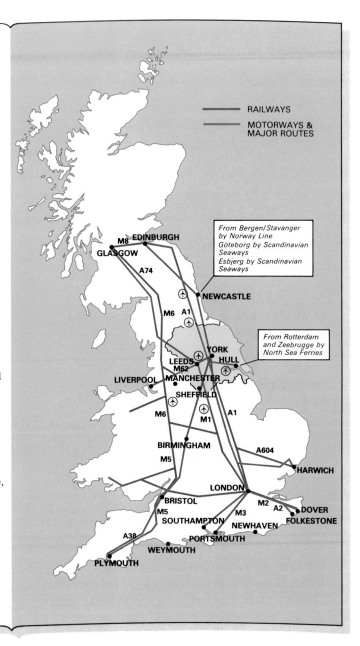

Summary

Best time of year:
Types of venue on offer:
Other attractions:
Getting there:

Writing

Using the text above as a model, write a passage promoting your town or region as a centre for conferences. Start by making notes about any special features you want to mention.

Activity

Work in pairs, one as the conference organizer for Moriati International, the other as the conference manager of the Twin Spires Hotel.

Conference organizer, Moriati International

You are trying to arrange a conference for Moriati International. Study the company's requirements, then find out about the conference facilities at the Twin Spires Hotel.

```
1 meeting room for 200
    theatre-style - 5 days

1 meeting room for 40
    classroom-style - 3 days

2 rooms for board meetings
    (15 each) - 2 days

2 video recorders

3 cordless microphones

1 stage for main room

1 overhead projector and screen

2 secretaries
```

Conference manager, Twin Spires

Study the table showing conference rooms and facilities at the Twin Spires Hotel. Try to persuade the conference organizer from Moriati International to hold his company's conference in your hotel.

TWIN SPIRES HOTEL

International Conference Service

Capacities	Ballroom	Churchill Room	Chaplin Room	Keaton Room
Theatre	350	100	50	40
Classroom	150	40	20	40
Board Room	110	35	16	18
Price per day	£ 700	£ 300	£ 250	£ 220

Equipment
We can supply stages, lecterns, overhead projectors, 35 mm. slide projectors, video recorders.

Support services
Full support services, including photographers and interpreters, are available.

Was the conference manager helpful?
Does the Twin Spires satisfy all your requirements?
How much is the hire of the rooms going to be?

Summary

Now you can

- Describe conference facilities
  The room holds 200 people theatre-style.
  We can arrange full support services.

- Use *too* and *enough* with adjectives
  This room is probably too small/not big enough for 40 people.

- Promote your region/country as a conference location

New words

applicant	interview
Autocue	meeting room
back projection	motorway
checklist	overhead projector
classroom-style	personality
commitment	promote
conference	screen
contractor	seminar
cordless microphone	summary
delegate	syndicate room
equipment	theatre-style
hire	venue
interpreter	video recorder

Listening 1

Listen to the guide explaining how Bordeaux wine is made and fill in the spaces in the passage. You may need more than one word.

First, the grapes . . . This is done by hand here, although some estates use machines. The grapes . . . then . . . and brought to the vathouse.

Here in the vathouse the grapes are . . . in a special machine and the juice . . . extracted.

After extraction, the juice goes into these vats, which . . . of stainless steel. It is essential that these vats are absolutely clean, or the wine can be ruined. The process of fermentation then begins.

When the fermentation is complete, the wine . . . to wooden casks, or *barriques*. If you follow me, we will visit the cellars where the casks are . . .

After about a year, the impurities . . . drawn to the bottom of the casks in a process known as 'fining'. The wine remains in the casks for a further period of between six months and a year and . . . to Bordeaux to be bottled.

Now, if you would like to return with me to the reception area, you can taste some of the wine produced on this estate.

Language study 1

The passive voice

When we say what people and things do, we use the active voice (e.g. *Tony works for British Rail, I asked a question*, etc.). When we are more interested in the result than in who or what does the action, we use the passive voice.

We often use the present simple passive to talk about processes (e.g. wine making). We form it with *is/are* + the past participle.

*The grapes **are taken** to the vathouse.*
*The wine **is transferred** to wooden casks.*

Practice A

Write down the past participle of these verbs.

Example: sing – *sung*

1   drive
2   begin
3   choose
4   ride
5   stand
6   feel
7   fall
8   deal with
9   lead
10   forget
11   cost
12   dive

Practice B

Rewrite these sentences using the present simple passive of the verb in brackets.

Example: People make chocolate from cocoa beans.
Chocolate ...
Chocolate is made from cocoa beans.

1   We request customers not to smoke. Customers ...
2   They speak English in Australia. English ...
3   We include service in the price. Service ...
4   They produce most of the world's rubber in Malaysia. Most ...
5   We serve meals throughout the day. Meals ...

Listening 2

Listen to the Mexican tour guide's description and then answer the questions below.

1   What does the tour guide say first?
2   Why are the wells important to Chichen Itza?
3   What shape is El Castillo?
4   When was it built?
5   What's on the upper platform?
6   What's inside the pyramid?

Language study 2

We form the past simple passive with *was/were* + the past participle.

The pyramid **was built** *in the 12th century.*
A tunnel **was opened**.
Another construction **was discovered** *directly underneath.*

Practice C

Put the verbs in these sentences into the past passive.

1 The temple . . . from local stone. (build)
2 The ruins . . . in the 18th century. (discover)
3 Extensive excavations . . . in the 1930s. (make)
4 The site . . . to tourists in 1948. (open)
5 The holiday . . . by bad weather. (spoil)
6 The flight . . . by three hours. (delay)

Practice D

The Colosseum in Rome is even more ancient than Chichen Itza. Now complete the verbs in the passage below which describes the history of the building.

The Colosseum . . . (begin) by the Emperor Vespasian between AD 70–76 and . . . (complete) by Titus in AD 80. During the 100-day opening festival many gladiators and 5000 wild animals . . . (kill). In the fifth century gladiatorial combats . . . (suppress), and 100 years later animal fights . . . (discontinue). Later the building . . . (damage) by a series of earthquakes and by the 15th century it . . . regularly . . . (use) as a source of building material for many great Roman buildings, including St. Peter's Basilica. This destruction . . . (stop) by Pope Benedict XIV and over the next century the massive amphitheatre . . . (restore). Gradually, the streets and buildings enclosing the arena . . . (demolish), so by 1933 the Colosseum was much as it appears today at the end of the Via dei Fori Imperiali.

Reading

Read the passages below and answer the questions which follow.

To experience the true magic of Kenya, a wildlife safari is unbeatable. The thrill of viewing wild animals in their natural habitat, of spending nights under starry African skies, and of achieving a closeness with nature you would not have thought possible, makes this an unforgettable holiday. Select from three safaris designed to cater for both first-timers and those returning to discover more of Africa.

Kenya appears in many tourist brochures. The Kenyan government has made tourist development a priority. It has spent money on building hotels, airports, safari lodges and all the other requirements for tourists from developed countries. The planes landing at Nairobi airport bring rich tourists from Europe, North America and Japan. Some come for Kenya's fine beaches. Most are more interested in the wildlife of East Africa. Lions, cheetahs, elephants and hippopotamuses are among the attractions.

Kenya's tourist industry earns the country over £200 million per year, but tourism does bring problems for a developing country.

- Only 75 per cent of the money spent by tourists stays in Kenya. The rest is taken by foreign companies which provide the hotels and the safaris.
- The tourist drinks Scotch whisky or Russian vodka. The hotels are fitted with American air-conditioning and Japanese lifts. The electrical system is Dutch and the fire control system is Italian. The safari vehicles are Japanese Land Cruisers. These imports cost Kenya vital foreign exchange.
- Kenya borrowed money from overseas to pay for the tourist developments, and much of the profits from tourism are spent in repaying the loans.
- There have been several armed attacks on tourists. The bad publicity hit Kenya's tourist earnings because people were frightened off. It is risky to become over-dependent upon tourism.

Most of the jobs created for Kenyans are unskilled and poorly paid. Some complain that tourism is a new form of colonialism. Tourism has also come into conflict with Kenya's rapid population growth. More mouths to feed means more demand for farmland. Already some Kenyans are demanding that the National Parks be opened up for farming.

1 Why are tourists attracted to Kenya for a holiday?
2 What advantages are provided for Kenya by tourism?
3 What problems are created by tourism for a country like Kenya?

Discussion

What are the positive and negative effects of tourism on your country or region? Are you optimistic about the future?

Activity

Work in pairs. Use local tourist maps and brochures to prepare a talk on a tourist attraction of your choice (e.g. a monument, building, industry, or craft). Use the passive where appropriate. Present your talk to another pair, or to the class.

Summary

Now you can

- Use the simple present and simple past passive
  The grapes are pressed in a special machine.
  The site was opened to tourists in 1948.

- Act as a tour guide
  Gather round everybody. Can you hear me at the back?

- Talk about the effects of tourism on your country

New words

amphitheatre	monument
ancient	process
arena	pyramid
attraction	rubber
basilica	ruins
cask	safari
cellar	temple
estate	tunnel
excavations	vathouse
extraction	well
fermentation	wildlife
festival	wine
hippopotamus	wooden

Listening

Listen to the tour operator representative explaining the tour from Bangkok to Malaysia and complete this tour diary.

Day 1 **Arrival in Bangkok**
You arrive in Bangkok and transfer to your hotel.

Day 2 **Bangkok**
You are free to . . . in your hotel or . . . the city.

Day 3 **Bangkok**
After visiting the . . . . . . in the morning, we spend the afternoon touring the Grand Palace and watching the display of Thai . . . In the evening, we take the overnight . . . to Nakorn Sri Thammarat.

Day 4 **Nakorn Sri Thammarat/Krabi**
On arrival, we visit the 7th century . . . and the museum, before going on to see the famous . . . at work. After lunch we drive to Krabi on the . . . coast.

Day 5 **Krabi/Phuket**
After . . . the night in Krabi, we set off early for Phuket. The rest of the day is yours to enjoy on Thailand's . . . island.

Day 6 **Phuket/Penang**
We take the early flight to Penang for the . . . part of the tour. You are free to explore the . . . . . . and mosques of Penang, or relax on the . . .

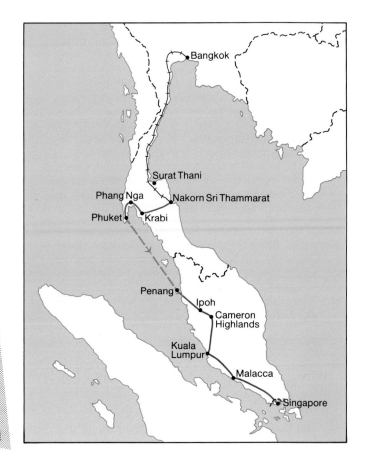

Language study 1

We often use the present simple tense to talk about timetables and programmes in the future.

*On day 1 you **arrive** in Bangkok and transfer to your hotel. On day 6 we **take** an early flight to Penang.*

Practice A

Work in pairs, one as a travel agent, the other as a tourist. Use the present simple to ask and answer questions about this day trip from London to Oxford and Woodstock.

08.15   Coach departs from London, Victoria.
10.00   Arrival in Oxford.
10.15   Tour of Oxford University colleges.
12.45   Lunch at the Turf Tavern.
14.00   Coach leaves for Woodstock.
14.30   Tour of Woodstock and Blenheim Palace.
17.30   Coach departs for London.

Example: **A**   *Where do we have lunch?*
            B   *You have lunch at the Turf Tavern.*

Remember to convert times to the twelve-hour clock.

Language study 2

These ways of joining sentences are common in itineraries.

***After spending** the night at Krabi, we set off early for Phuket.* (We spend the night at Krabi. Then we set off early for Phuket.)

*We see the 7th century temple and the museum, **before visiting** the famous silversmiths.* (We see the 7th century temple. Then we visit the famous silversmiths.)

Practice B

Join the following pairs of sentences using *after . . . ing*.

1   You arrive early in Bangkok. Then you are free to relax and explore the city.
2   We visit the Chinese Theatre. Then we spend the rest of the day at Disneyland.
3   We have breakfast in Queenstown. Then we take a flight over Mount Cook.

Practice C

Join the sentences below using *before . . . ing*.

1   We spend the morning in Moscow. Then we reboard the Orient Express.
2   You stay overnight in Agra. You visit the Taj Mahal the following morning.
3   You can stroll around Sydney. Then you can take a leisurely harbour cruise.

Reading

Special interest holidays are becoming increasingly popular as an alternative to the more traditional vacations. Read the brochure extracts below. Which holiday appeals to you more?

WHALE WATCHING IN ALASKA

Keep your eyes open and your cameras ready as you cruise among the San Juans, which provide the best opportunities in the world for viewing killer whales. We've chosen the best place and time for these fabulous creatures.
You'll stand at the bow, astonished and speechless, studying these individualistic animals cavorting and feasting on salmon. You'll get to know individual orcas and their family relationships, and learn their vocalizations – an enriching experience far more rewarding than merely 'seeing' the whales. Your intimate encounters will be a highly personal and emotional experience, a unique entree to the world of the orca!

Painting in Kashmir

This holiday is designed to offer you leisurely painting time in some of India's most spectacular scenery.
The architecture and scenery alone as subject matter are a painter's delight, but this trip will also provide you with an insight into the varied cultures and people of this wonderfully mysterious and romantic country. During the scorching summers of the northern plains, Moghul emperors retreated to the far more pleasant climes of Kashmir. Of the green valleys and wild flowers on the slopes, a poet said, 'If there is a paradise on earth, it is this, it is this, it is this.'

Activity

Breathtaking scenery – *fascinating* cities – *spectacular* caves

It is important to use a wide variety of adjectives when writing promotions. Which adjectives best describe the places shown below? Make a list for each picture.

Writing

1 Write a short tour diary (three or four days) around places of interest in your region or country.

2 Use the map and notes to make a short bus tour of Scotland. Allow one hour's travelling time per 50 km. Do not try to include everything.

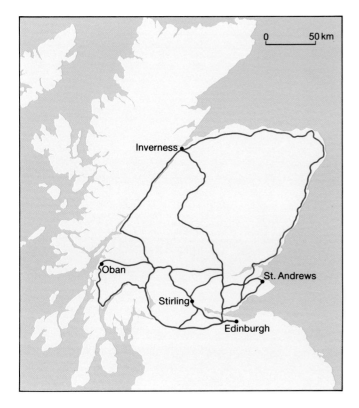

Place	Time required for visit	Points of interest
Edinburgh	two days	capital of Scotland / 12th century castle / royal palace of Holyroodhouse
Stirling	half day	historic town / famous castle / wildlife park
St Andrews	half day	ruined castle / ancient university/ beach / golf course
Inverness	one day	'the heart of the Scottish Highlands' / shopping for souvenirs
Oban	half day	harbour / nearby island of Mull (1 day) / scenery

3 Write an outline for a special interest holiday. Try to include as many details as possible (e.g. who, what, why, where, when, how much?).

Summary

Now you can

▪ Talk about planned programmes and tours
We leave at 11 a.m.
On day 3 we visit the famous floating market.

▪ Plan and write short tour diaries
After spending the night at Krabi, we set off early for Phuket.
You can explore the street markets, or spend the day on the beach.

New words

architecture	plain
cave	scenery
cavort	silversmith
culture	slope
delight	souvenir
display	tavern
leisurely	whale

Listening

Listen to this conversation in a Rome travel agency and answer these questions.

1 Why is the woman in Rome?
2 What does she want the travel agent to do?
3 Has the woman been to Florence before?
4 Why does she have to be in Venice on the Wednesday?

Language study 1

One of the uses of the present perfect tense is to ask or talk about experiences. In such cases we are not particularly interested in *when* something happened. We form the present perfect with *have* + the past participle.

Have *you ever* ***been*** *to Florence?*
I've never ***visited*** *Tuscany.*
I've ***seen*** *very little of Italy.*
We've already ***booked*** *tickets.*

Practice A

Match these questions and answers. Write an answer for **f**.

1 Have you ever eaten snake meat?
2 Have you read any good books recently?
3 Have you ever been to New Zealand?
4 Have you ever flown first class?
5 Have you been ill recently?
6 Have you ever ridden a motorcycle?

a Yes. I tried some in Thailand last year. I quite enjoyed it.
b No, I haven't. But I'd like to go there some time.
c Yes. That's how I get to work every day!
d No. I've been too busy the last couple of weeks.
e Yes, once. The company paid.
f . . .

Practice B

Write down three exciting or unusual things you have done in your life. Has anyone else in your class done the same as you? Ask and find out.

Language study 2

Compare the use of the past tense. Remember, we use the past tense to talk about activities which happened at a specific time in the past.

A *I* ***went*** *to the cinema yesterday.*
B *Which film* ***did*** *you see?* (They are still talking about yesterday.)

Practice C

Find out what your partner has and hasn't done. Make up dialogues starting *Have you ever tried . . ./been to . . ./seen . . .?* etc.

Example: A *Have you ever tried raw fish?*
          B *Yes, I have. (No, I haven't.)*
          A *When did you try it?*
          B *When I went to Japan.*

"Have you ever tried human?"

Itineraries

Reading

Read the letter and itinerary that the travel agency
FAXed to Mrs Munro. Suggest times when Mrs
Munro and Miss Parker could go on the excursions.
Are there any excursions they will not be able to take?

Dear Mrs Munro

Here is a suggested itinerary for your trip to Florence and Venice.

Can you come into the office tomorrow to collect your tickets and to settle your account?
Please note that I will need to take your credit card number to guarantee the hotel bookings.

ITINERARY FOR MRS MUNRO AND MISS PARKER

| Saturday, 5 April | Depart Rome (Termini) | 11.00 |
| | Arrive Florence | 13.10 |

Hotel Brunelleschi, via della Scala 7

Excursions
Florence city tour and Pitti Palace - afternoon, Mon-Fri
Pisa - morning, Tues, Thur, Sat
Siena and San Gimignano - full day, Mon, Wed, Fri

Tuesday, 8 April	Depart Florence	14.51
	Arrive Bologna	15.42
	Depart Bologna	16.44
	Arrive Venice	18.44

Hotel Londra Palace, Riva degli Schiavoni

Excursions
City tour and gondola ride - morning, daily
Venetian islands - morning, daily
Evening gondola serenade - 1 hour, daily

Saturday, 12 April	Depart Venice	10.25
	Arrive Bologna	12.23
	Depart Bologna	12.42
	Arrive Rome (Termini)	16.05

Yours sincerely

Carla Silvestrini

Carla Silvestrini

Activity

Mr Rossi is on a business trip in Linz, Austria. He would like to extend his trip to visit Salzburg and Vienna. Look at the notes and timetables. Then make up a suitable itinerary for Mr Rossi.

Notes

Mr Rossi wants to leave Linz on Monday 15 October. Must be back in Linz by 11 a.m., Friday 19 October at the latest. Would like to spend at least two days in each city. Wants information on excursions. Has arranged a business meeting in Vienna on 17 October at 11.00 a.m.

Hotels:

Hotel Elefant, Sigmund Haffnergasse 4, Salzburg.
Hotel Ananas, Rechte Wienzelle 101, Vienna.

Excursions, Salzburg:

City tour (Mozart's house, Mirabelle Palace) – daily, mornings.
Lakes and Mountains – daily, full day.

Excursions, Vienna:

City tour – daily, half day.
Vienna Woods and concert – Tuesday, Thursday, Saturday.

VIENNA - LINZ - SALZBURG

Vienna	dep.	0700	0800	0838	1000	....	1200	1300	1400	1504
Linz	arr.	0852	0954	1022	1152	....	1352	1452	1552	1657
Linz	dep.	0854	0956	1024	1154	1210	1354	1452	1552	1657
Salzburg	arr.	1015	1120	1137	1320	1400	1515	1615	1715	1825
Salzburg	dep.	0650	0812	0940	1040	1140	1240	1340	1440	1540
Linz	arr.	0759	0923	1101	1201	1301	1401	1501	1601	1540
Linz	dep.	0801	0925	1103	1203	1303	1403	1501	1601	1700
Vienna	arr.	0938	1105	1300	1400	1500	1600	1700	1800	1900

Summary

Now you can

▪ Use the present perfect tense to ask and talk about experiences
Have you ever been to Venice?
No. In fact I've seen very little of Italy.

▪ Plan and write an itinerary

New words

daily	serenade
gondola	settle an account
guarantee	snake
lake	Venetian
raw	woods

LAKIS TOURS
CAR HIRE SERVICE

All prices are in drachmas

Group	Type of car	Low	High
A	Suzuki SS40	40,200	46,900
B	Ford Fiesta Fiat Uno Suzuki GL30 Subaro	46,900	49,580
C	Nissan Cherry Opel Corsa	48,240	52,260
D	Beach Buggy	60,300	67,000
E	Suzuki 4x4	67,000	71,020

Low season: 1 Jan - 31 March
These prices include unlimited mileage, comprehensive insurance, and government tax of 20%. CDW (Collision Damage Waiver) insurance is available at an extra cost of 6,000 drs per week. Personal insurance is also available. Drivers must be over 21 and have held a full driving licence for at least 1 year.

Listening

Listen to this tourist in Greece enquiring about car rental and answer these questions.

1   What is the advantage of CDW insurance?
2   Has the tourist driven on the right before?
3   Why are there no group A or B cars available?
4   How much will the tourist have to pay in total?

Language study

We use the present perfect to talk about something that began in the past and is still the same now.

Present perfect + *for* + a period of time

We've been very busy for the last month or so.

Present perfect + *since* + specific point in time

I haven't driven on the right since I was in France.

Practice A

Work in pairs. Take turns to be **Student A** and **B**.

Student A
Form questions from the prompts below. Find out about your partner.

Student B
Give two short answers to these questions, one starting with *For*, the other with *Since*.

Example: How long/live/your present address?
       A *How long have you lived at your present address?*
       B *For nine months./Since August.*

1 How long/know/your best friend?
2 How long/have/your watch?
3 How long/be able to swim?
4 How long/be interested in tourism?

Practice B

Complete these sentences with the present perfect and *for* or *since*.

1 Paula . . . (have not) a holiday . . . (for/since) last summer.
2 I . . . (have) a driving licence . . . (for /since) April.
3 Marie . . . (not have) a driving accident . . . (for/since) she was in Spain.
4 We . . . (not see) Henri . . . (for/since) Tuesday.
5 They . . . (not take) an exam . . . (for/since) last May.
6 I . . . (not study) so hard . . . (for/since) a long time.
7 These students . . . (be) here . . . (for/since) four years.
8 I . . . (not see) our English teacher . . . (for/since) last week.

Practice C

Complete the following sentences using the simple past or present perfect of the verb in brackets.

1 Mr Granger . . . (be) in Crete since Saturday.
2 He . . . (live) in Italy for many years until he moved to the USA.
3 They . . . (arrive) in London on Friday.
4 Alan . . . (know) Barbara since 1988.
5 She . . . (pay) the balance of her account last week.
6 He . . . (not stop) talking since we arrived.
7 Mr and Mrs Black . . . (leave) on Thursday.
8 The tour . . . (finish) at 5 o'clock.

Reading

You work in a travel agency. Look at these customer enquiries about sports facilities at Club Med.

1   I'm not very good at sports. Is that going to be a problem?
2   What watersports are available?
3   Are you sure the instructors know what they're doing?
4   I like sport, but I burn very easily in the sun. Do Club Med run any indoor or evening activities?

Now read the information on Club Med sports facilities, then answer the enquiries with a full sentence.

Club Med

SUMMER 90

Sports ... If you come for a fortnight of non-stop activity you'll be spoilt for choice. But that doesn't mean you have to be bionic to begin with. In all our sporting pursuits we cater for inability as much as ability.

La fête du sport ... Play to win or play for fun, everything's possible.

Swimming	Sailing
Windsurfing	Water-skiing
Kayak	Fishing
Scuba diving	Snorkelling
Tennis	Football
Golf	Volleyball
Archery	Cycling
Riding	Body-building

and much much more ...

Sports instruction ... If you want to learn a sport, Club Med is the place. Our instructors are fully qualified to teach an enormous range of activities, from windsurfing to scuba diving, body-building to archery. If you are already très sportif they'll help you perfect your style.

Sports equipment ... We've got 8,000 tennis racquets to go round (and they've all got strings attached!). Most villages have several courts – Sandpiper in Florida has nineteen – and they are often floodlit for night games. In fact, Club Med is the biggest sports club in the world and we're proud of our vital statistics (118,200 golf balls, 25,000 arrows, 15,600 scuba flippers, 1,500 surfboards ...).

Activity 1

Look at the reading section again and choose at least five sports that you would like to try on this kind of holiday. Then, with a partner, act out a conversation between a customer and a travel agent.

Customer
Tell the travel agent which sports you are interested in.

Travel agent
Find out which sports the customer wants, then use the information in the chart below to advise him/her on the most suitable resort(s).

RESORT	MAJORCA		IBIZA		COSTA DEL SOL	TENERIFE	TUNISIA	YUGOSLAVIA	TURKEY
CLUB	SOL	PLAYA BLANCA	PEGASO	SAN MARCOS	PLAYA MARISOL	TURICOSTA	SUNMED	JUPITER	TOPKAPI
SWIMMING-POOL	●	●	●	●	●	●	●	●	●
SCUBA DIVING	●		●			●			●
TENNIS	●	●	●	●	●		●	●	●
GOLF	●	●		●	●			●	
ARCHERY	●	●	●	●		●	●		●
WATER-SKIING			●	●			●		●
FISHING				●				●	●
WINDSURFING	●	●	●	●			●	●	●
SAILING	●	●	●	●	●		●	●	●
RIDING	●	●				●	●	●	
VOLLEYBALL	●	●	●	●	●		●	●	●
SNORKELLING	●		●			●	●	●	●
CYCLING	●		●	●		●	●	●	●

Activity 2

Use the car hire brochure on page 80 to make up a conversation between a tourist and a car hire agent.

Tourist
You got your driving licence two years ago but you have only driven small cars. You plan to spend a week driving in the mountains. Try to hire the jeep.

Agent
Find out: how long the tourist has had a full licence.
            if he/she has ever driven a jeep.
Advise the tourist to take out CDW insurance.

Summary

Now you can

- Deal with car hire enquiries
  The price includes unlimited mileage, insurance, and government tax.
  Will you be the only driver?

- Use the present perfect with *for* and *since*
  We've been busy for the last month or so.
  I haven't driven on the right since I was in France.

- Talk about sports equipment hire

New words

accident	kayak
archery	mileage
arrow	pursuit
bionic	rental
body-building	riding
flippers	snorkelling
floodlit	surfboard
fortnight	water-skiing
inclination	

Listening

1 Read the advertisement below, then listen to this extract from an interview. Note down any information about the job which is not in the advertisement.

2 Do you think Anna will get the job? Give reasons for your answer.

HOTEL CONTRACTING
Assistant Contracts Manager

- Are you fluent in French and/or Spanish?
- Do you have experience in contracting, or a good knowledge of the hotel trade?
- Are you prepared to be based in London, but spend 50% of your time abroad?

Then call or write to:

**David Ansell,
Intertours Europe,
276 Brompto**
London SW
Tel. 071-80

CURRICULUM VITAE

Personal Details

Name	Anna Gourdin
Age	25
Address	169 Corkhill Place, London N1 1LR
Telephone	071 690 3999
Nationality	French

Language study

To talk about 'unreal' or imagined situations, we use the past tense in the *if-* clause, and *would* + infinitive in the main clause.

*At the end of six months, if we **felt** you **were** ready, we **would** allow you more independence.*

Sometimes the *if*-clause is implied but not expressed.

*Does that mean **I would** have to work alone?* (if I got the job)
*To start with you **would** work with the Contracts Manager.* (if you got the job)

Practice A

Complete these sentences.

1 If he . . . (have) more experience, I would offer him the job.
2 I . . . (apply) for another job if my qualifications were better.
3 If you . . . (work) harder, I'm sure you would pass.
4 If you came to Florence, I . . . (take) you round the sights.
5 What would you do if they . . . (offer) you the job?
6 I think she . . . (come) if you invited her.

Practice B

What would you do if:

you saw someone stealing food from a shop?
you found a wallet full of money on a bus?
you accidentally broke an expensive vase in a shop (but nobody saw you do it)?
a friend borrowed some money from you but forgot to repay you?

Begin your answers with *I would* . . .

Now make four similar questions to ask your partner.

Practice C

Imagine what it would be like to be:

a safari leader
a conference interpreter
a politician
a teacher
a model

What qualities would you need? Think of three things for each job, then tell your partner.

Example: a politician
            *You would have to be good at speaking in
            public.*

Reading

1 Read the article below. Then, in pairs, try to think of the most appropriate title.

The pattern for the development of the travel industry towards the year 2000 has been set. Quality, not quantity is the message. What this really means is giving people what they want, but asking them to pay for it.

Today's holidaymakers are very much more aware of their rights. They are no longer prepared to put up with sub-standard service, even when prices are low. In any case, recent research has shown that price is no longer the main priority when deciding on a holiday. Most people would rather pay that bit extra for the holiday they really want than take a second-rate package deal.

Self-catering arrangements are much in demand because they allow people the opportunity to be more selective about what they spend their time and money doing. Long-haul destinations and specialist holidays are also becoming increasingly popular.

For the retailer there is bad news and good. Falling volumes mean fewer customers. But those who do come through the door are likely to be prepared to spend more money on a better holiday.

This trend will mean that agents move away from being mere order-takers towards being proper travel consultants. As clients become more demanding – and more prepared to pay for quality – it will pay agents to spend a little more time getting it right.

2 Give some examples of long-haul destinations and specialist holidays.
3 Do you agree with the suggestion that agents at the moment are 'mere order-takers'?

Discussion

The year 2000 is not far away. How do you think the travel industry will change between now and then? First discuss your ideas with your partner, then with the rest of the class.

Writing

Look at Anna's letter of application. Has she referred to all the requirements mentioned in the advertisement?

16th March 1991   169 Corkhill Place,
London N1 1RL.

David Ansell,
Intertours Europe,
276 Brompton Close,
London SW9 6AB.

Dear Mr Ansell,
    I wish to apply for the position of Assistant Contracts Manager, advertised in the Travel Gazette on 14th March.
    As you will see from the enclosed curriculum vitae, I spent two years working for Thomsons as an on-site representative in Tunisia and Turkey. During this period I gained an intimate knowledge of the hotel industry in both countries and I feel I am ready for this new challenge.
    At present I am doing the English for Tourism course at Westminster College.
    French is my first language, but I also speak Spanish quite fluently.
    I look forward to hearing from you.

       Yours sincerely,

       A. Gourdin

       Anna Gourdin

Now write a similar letter applying for a job of your choice. You may invent work experience and qualifications.

Activity

Work in pairs or small groups. Choose one of the jobs below, or invent a job that would interest you. Then prepare for an interview. One person should be the applicant, the other(s) the interviewer(s).

Applicant

Write a short CV. If necessary, invent the qualifications and experience which you think you would need for the job. Try to imagine the questions you will be asked and prepare answers. You must give your CV to the interviewer(s) at the start of the interview.

Interviewer(s)

Prepare a description of the job you have chosen. You will have to invent some details. Make a list of questions to ask the applicant. Ask to see his/her CV at the start of the interview. Find out more about the applicant's qualifications and experience.

ARE YOU UP TO THE CHALLENGE?

Trek leaders wanted for Asia and Africa. Trek/tour experience essential. Foreign languages an advantage.

Business Travel

AZ always has career opportunities for travel consultants with Galileo, Travicom, or Sabre experience. We can advise you on jobs with a future. Salaries according to experience.

PERSONAL TRAVEL ADVISERS

Ours is the ultimate travel experience, offering discerning customers a service to suit their individual needs. We provide expert advice through private consultations.

Due to expansion, we have a vacancy for a Personal Travel Adviser. Excellent counselling and administration skills needed. Personality and appearance important.

Hotel Reservations

To join prestigious international hotel chain. 6 months' experience. Must speak one European language other than English.

Inbound Managers - from £16,000

Operations Managers for UK movements of foreign visitors. We are looking for French, Italian, Spanish, German, and Japanese speakers. Good organization skills and travel industry experience essential.

TOURISM

Summary

Now you can

▪ Use *would* to talk about hypothetical situations
To start with you would work with the Contracts Manager.
If we felt you were ready, we would allow you more independence.

▪ Take part in a job interview
I worked in Tunisia for the first year, then the following season I was transferred to Bodrum in Turkey.

▪ Talk about possible developments in the travel industry

▪ Write a letter of application

New words

assess	research
aware of	retailer
discerning	second-rate
in demand	selective
long-haul	self-catering
pattern	substandard
priority	travel consultant
progress	trek
qualification	vacancy
quality	volumes
report to	

Tapescripts

Unit 1

Interviewer: What sort of people come for lessons?

Instructor: Oh, all kinds – young and old, good and not so good. This group here are beginners, so I'm teaching them about the importance of safety. As you can see, they're practising in shallow water and staying close to the beach.

Interviewer: The weather must be a problem sometimes.

Instructor: Yes, it can be. Especially in winter. It gets very stormy around here. But then there are problems in the summer, too. Sometimes there's no wind at all.

Unit 2

Travel clerk: Good morning. Can I help you?

Tourist: Good morning. I want to book a flight from Barcelona to Rome.

Travel clerk: Yes, sir. When would you like to travel?

Tourist: Is there a flight on Friday evening?

Travel clerk: Friday evening ... Yes. Iberia fly to Rome on Friday evening.

Tourist: Oh, good. I've got an open round-the-world ticket, starting in New York.

Travel clerk: Have you got your ticket with you? There may be some restrictions.

Tourist: Sure. There you go.

Travel clerk: Thank you. Could you wait a minute while I check availability?

Tourist: Yes, sure.

Travel clerk: ... Yes, that's fine. There are no restrictions on this ticket. Can you give me your contact address and telephone number in Barcelona?

Tourist: Yes. It's the Hotel Goya and the number's ... 2018550.

Travel clerk: Fine. The flight leaves at half past eight. Would you please check in one hour before departure? Here's your ticket. Have a good flight.

Tourist: Thank you very much.

Unit 3

Travel agent: Good morning. Thai Travel. Can I help you?

Businessman: Good morning. I've got a flight reservation for Thursday, but I'd like to change it, please.

Travel agent: Certainly. What's your name please?

Businessman: Svenson, Arnold Svenson. That's S-V-E-N-S-O-N.

Travel agent: Where are you flying to?

Businessman: Tokyo.

Travel agent: Which flight are you on?

Businessman: The Thursday flight at 19.15.

Travel agent: And what's the flight number?

Businessman: It's TG 291.

Travel agent: When do you want to fly, sir?

Businessman: The same flight next week, that's a week on Thursday.

Travel agent: Same flight on Thursday, 16th April. Economy or Club Class, sir?

Businessman: Economy.

Travel agent: I'll just check availability ... Yes, that's confirmed. Would you like me to change any hotel bookings?

Businessman: No, I'm staying with friends. Thanks very much.

Travel agent: You're welcome. Thank you for calling.

Unit 4

Tourist: Good morning. I'd like some information on rail travel in the UK, please.

Travel agent: Certainly. Would you like to take a seat?

Tourist: Thank you. Right, well, I'm with my wife and son and we're planning to spend two weeks travelling around Britain. I'd like to know about tickets.

Travel agent: I recommend you buy the BritRail Pass. That gives you unlimited travel all over Britain.

Tourist: How long does it last?

Travel agent: Well, you want to travel for two weeks, so I suggest you buy the 15-day Pass. It's valid for eight days travel in a period of 15 days. It's good value.

Tourist: Hmm. What about children?

Travel agent: It depends on age. Children under five travel free. Those between five and sixteen travel for half price.

Tourist: Sounds great! How much is the adult fare . . .?

Unit 5

Traveller: Hello. I'd like some information about trains from Amsterdam to Paris, please.

Operator: Hold the line, please. I'll put you through to International Enquiries.

Clerk: International Enquiries. Can I help you?

Traveller: Yes. Can you tell me about trains from Amsterdam to Paris tomorrow?

Clerk: Certainly. What time would you like to leave?

Traveller: It doesn't really matter, but I have to be in Paris by 8.00 p.m.

Clerk: There's an express at 10.50, getting in at five past five.

Traveller: Hmm. I'd prefer to leave a bit later, I think.

Clerk: Well, the 12.26 arrives in Paris at 18.57, but you have to change in Brussels.

Traveller: The time is better, but I'd really rather not change. Is there a later train?

Clerk: There is, but you would still have to change.

Traveller: I see. In that case the 10.50 is probably the best. Can I buy a ticket now? I've got a credit card.

Unit 6

The tapescript for this unit is on p.28.

Unit 7

Enter the terminal by the Departures entrance. The Information Desk is in front of you. Turn left for domestic flights; turn right for the bank and the car hire office. The airport shops are on the left, opposite the airline desks. Turn right after the airline desks and you will see the check-in desk next to the lost property office. There is a café in the centre of the ground floor. Take the escalator or stairs to the first floor for the restaurant and bar.

When your flight is called, follow the signs to Departures and have your boarding card ready. Then go through passport control and airport security. You can visit the duty-free shop, on the right of the departure lounge, to buy tax-free goods. Then follow the corridor along to your departure gate.

Unit 8

Tourist: Oh, it's so hot! Phew! . . . Could you give me some information about the city? We've got a day's stopover for sightseeing.

Lucy Tan: Certainly, madam. This leaflet will give you plenty of ideas on what to see. It includes directions to all the main attractions.

Tourist: Hmm. What would you recommend?

Lucy Tan: If you're only here for a day, you ought to visit Chinatown – that's the old part of the city. Then in the afternoon you could always take a bus tour, or walk round the Botanic Gardens. And you should try to visit Raffles Hotel.

Tourist: That sounds like a busy day! What about places to eat?

Lucy Tan: Well, Singapore is full of restaurants, or you could eat at Newton Circus. That's an open-air food centre with stalls selling lots of different types of food.

Tourist: Mmm. You're making me hungry!

Lucy Tan: OK. Let me mark those places on this map. I suggest you travel by taxi. They're quite cheap, and of course they're air-conditioned.

Unit 9

Listening 1   The tapescript for this is on p.40.

Listening 2

1

Travel agent: So, including the single-room supplement, that comes to £645 altogether. Would you like to confirm?
Client: Yes, please.
Travel agent: Can I have your name, please?
Client: Yes, it's Kramer. Miss T Kramer.
Travel agent: Right. There's a deposit of £55 which is payable now.
Client: Fine. Can I pay by cheque?
Travel agent: Certainly. The balance of . . . £590 is due six weeks before you leave. If you wait just a moment, I'll get a printout of the details for you.

2

Tourist: I'd like to buy some French francs, please.
Cashier: Certainly, sir. What currency do you have?
Tourist: Pounds sterling.
Cashier: Very good. And how much would you like to change?
Tourist: I'm not sure. What's your exchange rate today?
Cashier: Er . . . It's exactly 9 francs to the pound. But we charge 2% commission on each transaction.
Tourist: I see. Then I'll change £100.
Cashier: Right . . . So that comes to 882 francs in total.
Tourist: OK. Thanks.

3

Guest: I'd like to check out, please. Can I have my bill?
Reception: Certainly, sir. What was your room number, please?
Guest: 523.
Reception: 523 . . . That's two nights with breakfast at corporate rate, plus dinner for two on the 22nd, room service, bar, and telephone. That's a total of 420,000 lire. How would you like to pay?
Guest: American Express?
Reception: That'll do nicely, sir. Could I have your card, please?

Unit 10

This country is in Europe. It's larger than Switzerland, but smaller than Italy. It's farther west than Bulgaria, and farther south than Austria. It's flatter in the south than in the north.

Unit 11

Lotus rep: So you've got a swimming-pool and a restaurant. Any other facilities?
General Manager: Not yet. But we're going to try to negotiate a deal with the watersports club so that our guests can use their facilities. And we're also going to build a poolside bar during the winter.
Lotus rep: Good idea. Now, let me see . . . You've got 120 rooms altogether, is that right?
General Manager: Yes. At the moment there are 120 rooms plus two suites, each with its own jacuzzi and private bar. Our twins and doubles are divided into two categories. There are some with balcony and beach view, and then there are a number of rooms with garden view.
Lotus rep: What about family rooms?
General Manager: We have eleven family rooms. At the end of this season we're going to start building an extension with thirty deluxe doubles.
Lotus rep: Mmm. I see. Are all the current rooms en suite?
General Manager: Yes. They've all got private bathrooms with bath and shower.
Lotus rep: Good. Are any of the rooms interconnecting?
General Manager: Yes. There are a number of interconnecting doubles on each floor. Twenty altogether.
Lotus rep: Right. Well perhaps we should go in and take a look at those rooms now. I think it's going to rain!
General Manager: Yes. I think you're right. Not a very good selling point!

Unit 12

Switchboard: Good morning. Mountjoy Hotel.

Caller: Good morning. Reservations, please.

Switchboard: One moment. I'll put you through.

Reservations: Reservations. Can I help you?

Caller: Yes, please. I'd like to book a single room for four nights from 10th August.

Reservations: Right. I'll just check that . . . Yes, madam. We can do that for you.

Caller: How much will that be, please?

Reservations: £65 per night, including full English breakfast.

Caller: That's for a room with bathroom?

Reservations: Yes, madam. All our rooms have private bathroom, colour television, radio, in-house video, telephone, and tea- and coffee-making facilities.

Caller: That's fine.

Reservations: Could I have your name, please?

Caller: The booking's for Mr Williams of Oliver Electronics, London.

Reservations: OK. That's a single room for four nights from 10th August. Would you confirm that by FAX or telex, please?

Caller: Yes, I'll do that. Mr Williams will probably arrive quite late. Can you hold the room until 10.00?

Reservations: Yes, of course.

Caller: Thank you. Goodbye.

Reservations: Goodbye.

Unit 13

Guest: Good evening. My name is Casado. I have a reservation.

Reception: Good evening, Mr Casado. Yes, we received your telex. A single room for two nights, leaving on 22nd December. Would you please fill in the registration form? I'll get your key.

Guest: Thank you.

Reception: Here is your keycard. Your room number is 807. Would you like dinner tonight?

Guest: Perhaps later.

Reception: Well, the hotel restaurant is open until 11.00 p.m. But if you want something to eat later than that, just call room service.

Guest: Good. Er . . . is Mr Archer here yet?

Reception: No, sir. Not yet. But I'll ask him to call you when he arrives. Will you be in your room?

Guest: Yes, I think so.

Reception: Certainly, sir. Now . . . the bellboy will show you to your room. Have a pleasant stay in Stockholm, sir!

Guest: Thank you.

Unit 14

1

Customer: My name is Sarah Ashton. I booked a flight to London through this office last week. It was a telephone booking and I paid by Visa. This morning I received the ticket and you've booked me on the wrong flight.

Travel agent: Hmm . . . What flight did you want?

Customer: I want to travel on the 10 a.m. flight tomorrow. This ticket is for the 14.00.

Travel agent: Are you sure you booked the 10 o'clock flight?

Customer: Look! I definitely booked the 10 o'clock flight!

Travel agent: Well, that's a special fare. If you want to change the departure time, there will be a charge to upgrade the ticket.

Customer: What! I don't believe this! Listen! This is your mistake! If you think I'm going to pay any more . . .

2

Guest: My name is Hagen. I'm in room 229. This morning I was woken up at 6 o'clock by a telephone call that wasn't for me. Now this is the second time this has happened. It's just not good enough! The call was for a Mr Haugen! Don't you people listen!

Reception: I'm most terribly sorry, Mr Hagen. I will inform the early morning supervisor. She will ensure it doesn't happen again.

Guest: Well, I hope not! Also, I received this FAX this morning. I've only got the first two pages. There should be four more. Didn't anyone check? This is a very important document!

Reception: I do apologize, Mr Hagen. I'll check the FAX office straight away. Could I have those two sheets, please?

Guest: Right . . .

Unit 15

Greta Mueller: Yes. As I said on the telephone, we're planning a three-day conference in April next year for about 150 people. Now, we'll need one large room for the main conference and three smaller rooms for round table discussions for around 40 delegates each.

Sales Manager: I see. Well, the ballroom is big enough to hold 200 theatre-style. We do have a number of rooms next door to the ballroom but they're probably a little too small for 40 people.

Greta Mueller: Hmm. But presumably you do have some other meeting rooms?

Sales Manager: Yes, we do. We can certainly accommodate you elsewhere in the hotel.

Greta Mueller: Fine. What about equipment?

Sales Manager: We can supply most things – video recorder, overhead projector, cordless microphones . . .

Greta Mueller: What about back projection and Autocue?

Sales Manager: Mm. No. I'm afraid not.

Greta Mueller: And support services – secretaries, interpreters, photographers?

Sales Manager: We can arrange full support services through an outside contractor.

Greta Mueller: Good. Will it be possible to get detailed room plans?

Sales Manager: Certainly. Our conference pack has all that sort of information, as well as a full list of our menus and room rates.

Unit 16

Listening 1   This tapescript is on page 68.

Listening 2

Guide: Gather round everybody. Form a semi-circle in front of me. Good, that's right. Now I hope you can all hear me. Can you hear me at the back? Good.

Now the ancient Mayan city of Chichen Itza is one of the most important archaeological sites in the world. In English the name means 'the mouth of the well of the Itza people'. The wells are of vital importance because there are no rivers in this part of Yucatan.

We will begin our tour here in the great central plaza with the pyramid of El Castillo, which you can see behind me. The pyramid was built in the Toltec period around the 12th century AD. It is 25 metres high and is made up of nine terraced platforms built on a square base. Each side of the pyramid is 60 metres long, with a stairway leading to the temple on the upper platform. When the floor of the temple was excavated, another construction was discovered directly underneath. A tunnel was opened and an inner pyramid made up of nine terraces was found.

Before we climb to the temple, I'd like to show you some of the decoration on the panels of the . . .

Unit 17

Tour operator representative:
Good morning. I'd like to welcome you on behalf of Thailand Tours to the Oriental Hotel, Bangkok. My name is Joanna and I'm your tour leader for the first part of your holiday.

I'm going to spend a few minutes outlining your 15-day overland tour to Singapore. If you have any questions, please don't hesitate to interrupt.

Day 2 – that's tomorrow – is a free day, so you may just want to relax in your hotel. But if you're feeling more energetic you could explore the city.

On day 3 we visit the famous floating market in the morning. Then we take a tour of the Grand Palace in the afternoon and later watch some Thai boxing. In the evening we take the overnight train to Nakorn Sri Thammarat.

On day 4 we stop at Nakorn Sri Thammarat to see the 7th century temple and the museum. Then we visit the famous local silversmiths at work. After lunch we drive to Krabi on the west coast where we have dinner and stay overnight.

On day 5 we set off early for Phuket where you can relax and enjoy Thailand's largest island.

The next day, day 6, we take the early morning flight to Penang for the Malaysian part of the tour. Again it's a free day, so you can explore the street markets, or spend the day relaxing on the beach.

Unit 18

Travel agent: Buon giorno, signora. Posso aiutarla?
Woman: Er, do you speak English?
Travel agent: Yes, madam. Can I help you?
Woman: Oh, good. Now, I'm here with a colleague for a conference, but we'd like to stay on afterwards and visit Florence and Venice. Do you think you could organize a trip for us and maybe suggest some excursions that we could go on?
Travel agent: Certainly, madam. It would be a pleasure. Could you give me your name, please?
Woman: Of course. My name is Mrs Munro and my colleague is Miss Parker.
Travel agent: Right. What date would you like to go?
Woman: Saturday, 5th April.
Travel agent: ... 5th April. Returning to Rome on ...?
Woman: Saturday, 12th.
Travel agent: Fine. Have you ever been to Florence?
Woman: No, I've never visited Tuscany. In fact, I've seen very little of Italy – except Rome.
Travel agent: Well, the best way to see Florence is on foot. The Duomo, the Palazzo Vecchio, the Uffizi and the Pitti Palace are all very central. But I can give you details of various excursions as well.
Woman: That's very kind. Now we must be in Venice on the Wednesday. We've already booked some concert tickets for that evening.
Travel agent: O.K. That's no problem. Perhaps you could look at these hotels and tell me which ones interest you. Then I can make up an itinerary and FAX it to your hotel.
Woman: Thank you.
Travel agent: Do you have a credit card?

Unit 19

Tourist: I'm thinking of hiring a car. Can you tell me about your rental terms?
Agent: Certainly. Here is our brochure. These are the weekly rates. They include unlimited mileage, insurance, and government tax of 20%.
Tourist: Hmm. What's the difference between Collision Damage Waiver insurance and ordinary insurance?
Agent: Well, the ordinary insurance does not cover you completely if you have an accident. You still have to pay the first 25,000 drachmas. The CDW insurance means you don't pay anything if you have an accident – even if it's your fault.
Tourist: Hmm. I must say, I'm a little worried. I haven't driven on the right since I was in France about five years ago ... and then I had an accident.
Agent: I see ...
Tourist: Oh, it wasn't my fault!
Agent: ... You do have a full clean licence ...?
Tourist: Yes.
Agent: OK. I'm afraid we don't have anything in Group A or B at the moment. We've been very busy for the last month or so. I can give you a Nissan Cherry.
Tourist: I suppose that will do.
Agent: Right. How long do you want to keep it?
Tourist: Two weeks, please, until 16 May, and I think I'll take out CDW insurance, too.
Agent: OK. Could I see your passport and licence, please? ... Thank you. Now, will you be the only driver?

Unit 20

Interviewer: Right, Anna. Let me tell you a little about the job first, and then you can tell me about yourself, all right?

Anna: Yes, fine.

Interviewer: Good. Well, the job title is Assistant Contracts Manager. Basically, it involves visiting hotels, assessing them according to our own rating system, and deciding if we should include them in our brochure. As the advertisement said, you would be based in London, but you would spend an equal amount of time abroad – France and Spain, mainly, but there would be some trips to Hungary and Bulgaria.

Anna: Mmm. Does that mean I would work alone?

Interviewer: No. To start with you would work with the Contracts Manager – you'll meet her later – er, but you wouldn't be directly involved in negotiating with hotels at that stage. However, at the end of six months we would assess your progress, and if we felt you were ready, we would allow you more independence. You would still report to the Contracts Manager, of course. Any questions so far?

Anna: No. I think that's clear.

Interviewer: Now I see from your CV that you spent two years working as a rep for Thomson, is that right?

Anna: Yes. I worked in Tunisia for the first year, then the following season I was transferred to Bodrum in Turkey. I got to know all the hotels quite well.

Interviewer: Yes. I wanted to ask you about that.

INFINITIVE	PAST TENSE	PAST PARTICIPLE	INFINITIVE	PAST TENSE	PAST PARTICIPLE
be	was	been	lend	lent	lent
beat	beat	beaten	let	let	let
become	became	become	lie	lay	lain
begin	began	begun	light	lit	lit
bend	bent	bent	lose	lost	lost
bite	bit	bitten	make	made	made
blow	blew	blown	mean	meant	meant
break	broke	broken	meet	met	met
bring	brought	brought	put	put	put
build	built	built	read	read	read
burn	burnt	burnt	ride	rode	ridden
buy	bought	bought	ring	rang	rung
catch	caught	caught	rise	rose	risen
choose	chose	chosen	run	ran	run
come	came	come	say	said	said
cost	cost	cost	see	saw	seen
cut	cut	cut	sell	sold	sold
dig	dug	dug	send	sent	sent
do	did	done	set	set	set
draw	drew	drawn	shake	shook	shaken
dream	dreamt	dreamt	shine	shone	shone
drink	drank	drunk	shoot	shot	shot
drive	drove	driven	shut	shut	shut
eat	ate	eaten	sing	sang	sung
fall	fell	fallen	sink	sank	sunk
feed	fed	fed	sit	sat	sat
feel	felt	felt	sleep	slept	slept
fight	fought	fought	slide	slid	slid
find	found	found	smell	smelt	smelt
fly	flew	flown	speak	spoke	spoken
forget	forgot	forgotten	spend	spent	spent
freeze	froze	frozen	stand	stood	stood
get	got	got	steal	stole	stolen
give	gave	given	stick	stuck	stuck
go	went	gone	strike	struck	struck
hang	hung	hung	swear	swore	sworn
have	had	had	swim	swam	swum
hear	heard	heard	take	took	taken
hide	hid	hidden	teach	taught	taught
hit	hit	hit	tear	tore	torn
hold	held	held	tell	told	told
hurt	hurt	hurt	think	thought	thought
keep	kept	kept	throw	threw	thrown
know	knew	known	understand	understood	understood
lay	laid	laid	wake	woke	woke/woken
lead	led	led	wear	wore	worn
lean	leant	leant	win	won	won
learn	learnt	learnt	write	wrote	written
leave	left	left			

This is the layout of a typical letter from a travel agency:

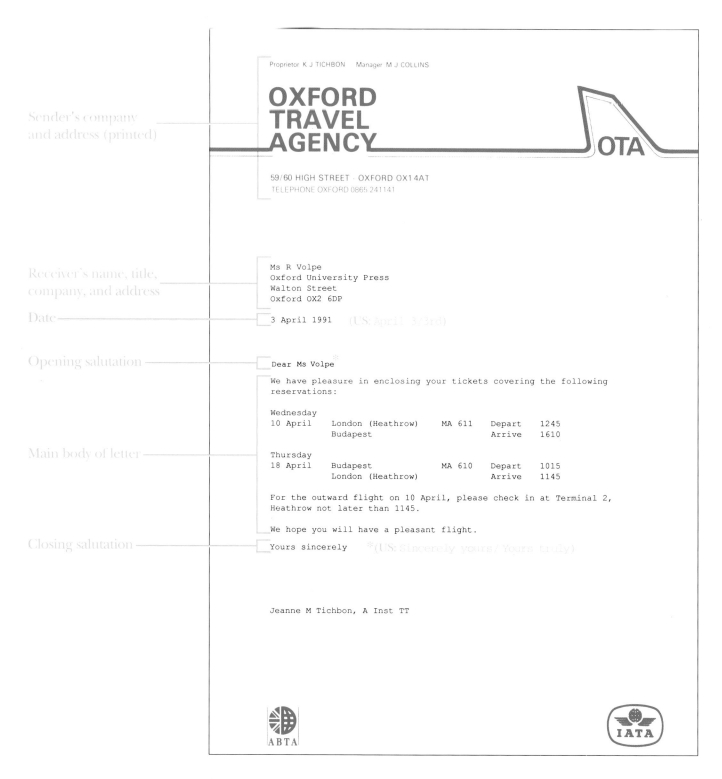

Sender's company and address (printed)

Proprietor K J TICHBON   Manager M J COLLINS

OXFORD TRAVEL AGENCY OTA

59/60 HIGH STREET · OXFORD OX1 4AT
TELEPHONE OXFORD 0865 241141

Receiver's name, title, company, and address

Ms R Volpe
Oxford University Press
Walton Street
Oxford OX2 6DP

Date

3 April 1991   (US: April 3/3rd)

Opening salutation

Dear Ms Volpe

Main body of letter

We have pleasure in enclosing your tickets covering the following reservations:

Wednesday
10 April   London (Heathrow)   MA 611   Depart   1245
            Budapest   Arrive   1610

Thursday
18 April   Budapest   MA 610   Depart   1015
            London (Heathrow)   Arrive   1145

For the outward flight on 10 April, please check in at Terminal 2, Heathrow not later than 1145.

We hope you will have a pleasant flight.

Closing salutation

Yours sincerely   *(US: Sincerely yours/Yours truly)

Jeanne M Tichbon, A Inst TT

ABTA

IATA

* Receiver's name known: Dear Rosa/Ms Volpe — Yours sincerely
Receiver's name not known: Dear Sir — Yours faithfully

Here are some common telex abbreviations:

about	ABT
above	ABV
and	N
as soon as possible	ASAP
available	AVAIL
charge	CHG
cheque	CHQ
confirm	CFM
could	CLD
date/dated	DT/DTD
delivery	DELY
department	DEPT
development	DEVT
double bedroom	DBLB
error	EEEE
for the attention of	ATTN
for your information	FYI
from	FM
have	HV
information	INFO
international	INTL
manager	MGR
message	MSG
payment	PYMT
please	PLS/PSE
quantity	QTY
re your letter	RYL
re your telex	RYT
receive/received	RCV/RCVD
regards	RGDS
repeat	RPT
required	REQD
return	RTN
service	SVC
should	SHD
single bedroom	SGLB
telephone conversation	TELECON
telex	TLX
thank you	TKU
thanks	TKS
very	V
would	WD
you	U
your	UR/YR

Word list

The translations below refer to words only as they are used in this book. The meanings of certain words will vary according to context.

ENGLISH/US ENGLISH	FRENCH	SPANISH	ITALIAN
abroad 5	à l'étranger	en el extranjero	all'estero
accident 19	accident	accidente	incidente
accommodation 6	logement	alojamiento	sistemazione
(US: accommodations)			
acknowledge 14	accuser réception	acusar recibo	confermare
administration costs 3	frais administratifs	costes/costos administrativos	spese amministrativie
adult 4	adulte	adulto	adulto
advance booking 7	réservation	reserva por adelantado	prenotazione anticipata
adventure 4	aventure	aventura	avventura
advertisement 11	publicité	anuncio	annuncio pubblicitario
advice 1	conseil	consejo	consiglio/consigli
airline 2	compagnie aérienne	línea aérea	linea aerea
airport security 7	service de sécurité des aéroports	seguridad de aeropuerto	sicurezza aeroportuale
aisle 4	couloir	pasillo	corridoio
alarm call 13	réveil par téléphone	llamada de alarma	sveglia
(US: wake-up call)			
allowed 6	autorisé	permitido	consentito
alter 3 (US: change)	modifier	modificar	cambiare
alteration 3	modification	enmienda	cambiamento
amendment 3 (US: change)	changement	corrección	correzione
amount 6	montant	cantidad	importo
amphitheatre 16	amphithéâtre	anfiteatro	anfiteatro
ancient 16	ancien	antiguo	antico
apologies 14	excuses	disculpas	scuse
apologize 4	excuser	pedir disculpas	scusarsi
applicant 15	candidat	solicitante	candidato
apply 6	faire une demande	solicitar	far domanda
appointment 2	rendez-vous	cita	appuntamento
archery 19	tir à l'arc	tiro con arco	tiro all'arco
architecture 17	architecture	arquitectura	architettura
arena 16	arène	pista	arena
arrange 1	planifier	organizar	organizzare
arrangement 1	plan	planes	piano/programma
arrow 19	flèche	flecha	freccia
assess 20	évaluer	evaluar	valutare
assistance 5	aide, assistance	servicio	assistenza
attraction 16	attraction	atracción/atractivo	attrazione
authority 12	autorité	autoridad	autorità
authorization 9	autorisation	autorización	autorizzazione
Autocue 15	téléprompteur	Autocue/chuleta	schermo di lettura
(US: Teleprompter)			
availability 2	disponibilité	disponibilidad de billetes	disponibilità
aware of 20	au courant de	ser consciente de	a conoscenza di
back projection 15	surimpression	con cabina de proyección	proiezione di fondo
(US: back-view projection)			
balance 6	solde	saldo	saldo
balcony 11	balcon	balcón	balcone
basilica 16	basilique	basílica	basilica
bay 8	baie	bahía	baia
beach 8	plage	playa	spiaggia
bill 9	note (addition)	cuenta	conto
bionic 19	bionique	biónico	bionico
blacklist 9	liste noire	lista negra	lista nera

Word list

ENGLISH/US ENGLISH	GERMAN	TURKISH	JAPANESE
abroad 5	im Ausland	yurtdışı	海外で／外国で
accident 19	Unfall	kaza	事故
accommodation 6	Unterkunft	konaklama	宿泊施設／宿泊設備
(US: accommodations)			
acknowledge 14	bestätigen	kabullenmek	承認する／認知する
administration costs 3	Verwaltungskosten	kayıt işlem masrafları	運営コスト／処理コスト
adult 4	Erwachsene(r)	yetişkin	成人
advance booking 7	Reservierung	yer ayırtma	予約
adventure 4	Abenteuer	serüven	冒険
advertisement 11	Reklame/Anzeige	reklam	広告／宣伝
advice 1	Rat/Ratschlag	tavsiye	忠告／助言
airline 2	Fluggesellschaft	hava yolları	航空会社
airport security 7	Flughafensicherung	havaalanı güvenliği	空港警備
aisle 4	Gang	koridor	（座席列間の）通路
alarm call 13	Weckruf	uyandırma servisi	目覚まし電話／モーニングコール
(US: wake-up call)			
allowed 6	erlaubt	müsaade edilme	許可された／許可されている
alter 3 (US: change)	ändern	değiştirmek	変更する
alteration 3	Änderung	değişme	変更
amendment 3 (US: change)	Änderung/Zusatz	ufak değişiklik	修正
amount 6	Betrag	tamamı	額／量
amphitheatre 16	Amphitheater	anfiteatr	（古代ローマの）円形劇場／円形競技場
ancient 16	alt	antik/çok eski	古代の
apologies 14	Entschuldigungen	özür dilemeler	謝罪／弁明
apologize 4	sich entschuldigen	özür dileme	謝罪する／弁明する
applicant 15	Bewerber(in)	başvuruda bulunan	志願者／申請人
apply 6	beantragen	başvuruda bulunmak	志願する／申請する
appointment 2	Termin	randevu/buluşma	面会の約束
archery 19	Bogenschießen	okçuluk	アーチェリー／洋弓術
architecture 17	Architektur	mimari	建築様式
arena 16	Arena	arena	闘技場／試合場
arrange 1	arrangieren	ayarlamak	手配する
arrangement 1	Planung	program	手配
arrow 19	Pfeil	ok	矢
assess 20	beurteilen	değerlendirmek	評価する
assistance 5	Hilfe	yardım	手伝い／助力
attraction 16	Attraktion	turistin ilgisini çeken	魅力／アトラクション／呼び物
authority 12	Autorität	otorite/üstünlük	権威／権力／影響力
authorization 9	Genehmigung	yetki verme	認可
Autocue 15	Autocue/Teleprompter	(televizyon) sufle bandı	オートキュー（講演者に台詞を教える電子装置）
(US: Teleprompter)			
availability 2	Verfügbarkeit	temin edilebilirlik	利用の可能性
aware of 20	bewußt	bilincinde	認識して／承知して
back projection 15	Rückprojektion	projeksiyon	バックグラウンド・プロジェクション
(US: back-view projection)			
balance 6	Restbetrag	bakiye	差額
balcony 11	Balkon	balkon	バルコニー
basilica 16	Basilika	bazilika	（古代ローマの）会堂
bay 8	Bucht	körfez	湾
beach 8	Strand	kumsal/plaj	浜辺／渚
bill 9	Rechnung	hesap (pusulası)	勘定書
bionic 19	bionisch	biyonik	生物工学的／並みの人間以上の力のある
blacklist 9	schwarze Liste	kara liste	ブラックリスト／注意人物一覧表

Word list

ENGLISH/US ENGLISH	FRENCH	SPANISH	ITALIAN
boarding card 7 (US: boarding pass)	carte d'embarquement	tarjeta de embarque	carta d'imbarco
body-building 19	musculation	culturismo	sviluppo muscolare
booking 1	réservation	reserva	prenotazione
brochure 2	brochure	folleto	opuscolo/dépliant
buffet car 4	wagon restaurant	coche-comedor	carrozza buffet
building 7	immeuble	edificio	edificio
bullring 8	arène	plaza de toros	arena (per corride)
business (adj.) 1	d'affaires	de negocios	di lavoro, d'affari
bustle 13	remue-ménage	bullicio	trambusto
calculate 9	calculer	calcular	calcolare
caller 12	personne qui appelle	comunicante	chiamante
camp site 1	terrain de camping	camping	campeggio
camper 1	campeur	campista	campeggiatore
cancel 2	annuler	suspender	annullare
cancellation charge 3	frais d'annulation	tarifa de cancelación	spese di annullamento
car hire office 7	bureau de location de voiture	oficina de alquiler de coches	ufficio noleggio auto
card holder 9	détenteur de la carte	titular de (la) tarjeta	intestatario della carta
cashier 9	caissier	cajero	cassiere/a
cask 16	tonneau, fût	tonel	botte
catamaran 8	catamaran	catamarán	catamarano
category 11	catégorie	clase	categoria
cause offence 14 (US: to offend)	offenser	ofender	recare offesa
cave 17	grotte	cueva	grotta
cavort 17	faire des gambades	dar cabrioladas/saltos	far capriole
cellar 16	cave	bodega	cantina
check in (verb) 2	enregistrer	facturar	presentarsi all'accettazione
check-in (adj.) 2	d'enregistrement	de factura	accettazione
checklist 15	checklist	lista (de chequeo)	lista di controllo
cheque 4 (US: check)	chèque	cheque	assegno
classroom-style 15	style salle de classe	estilo aula	tipo aula scolastica
client 6	client	cliente	cliente
cliff 8	falaise	acantilado	scogliera
closed 12	fermé	cerrado	chiuso
coastline 10	côte	línea costera	costa
commission 9	commission	comisión	provvigione
commitment 15	engagement	compromiso	impegno
complain 14	réclamation	quejarse	reclamare
complaint 14	faire une réclamation	queja	reclamo
comprehensive 9	tout risque	exhaustivo	globale
computer 2	ordinateur	ordenador	computer
conference 15	conférence	congreso	convegno
confirmation 12	confirmation	confirmación	conferma
confirmed 3	confirmé	confirmado	confermato
contact address 2	adresser/contacter quelqu'un	dirección	recapito
continental 4	européen (pour les Britanniques)	continental	continentale
contractor 15	entrepreneur	contratista	impresa
coral (adj.) 10	de corail	coralino	di corallo
cordless microphone 15	micro sans fil	micrófono sin cables	microfono senza filo
corridor 7	couloir	pasillo	corridoio
countryside 4	campagne	campo	campagna
couple 11	couple	pareja/matrimonio	coppia
cove 10	crique	cala	insenatura
cover (verb) 3	couvrir	cubrir	coprire
credit card 4	carte de crédit	tarjeta de crédito	carta di credito
cross-channel 4	trans Manche	que atraviesa la Mancha	che attraversa la Manica
cruise 8	croisière	crucero	crociera
cuisine 10	cuisine	cocina	cucina
culture 17	culture	cultura	cultura
currency 9	devise	moneda	valuta
customer 1	client	cliente	cliente

ENGLISH/US ENGLISH	GERMAN	TURKISH	JAPANESE
boarding card 7 (US: boarding pass)	Bordkarte	uçuş kartı	搭乗券
body-building 19	Bodybuilding	vücut geliştirme	ボディー・ビル
booking 1	Buchung	yer ayırtma	予約
brochure 2	Broschüre/Prospekt	broşür/kitapçık	パンフレット
buffet car 4	Speisewagen	yemekli vagon	軽食車車
building 7	Gebäude	bina	建物
bullring 8	Stierkampfarena	arena (boğa güreşi)	闘牛場
business (adj.) 1	Geschäfts-	iş	事業の
bustle 13	Betrieb	karmaşa	ざわめき／雑踏
calculate 9	berechnen	hesaplamak	計算する
caller 12	Anrufer(in)	arayan (telefonla)	電話をかける人
camp site 1	Zeltplatz	kamp yeri	キャンプ場
camper 1	Camper(in)	kampçı	キャンプする人／キャンパー
cancel 2	absagen	iptal etmek	取消す
cancellation charge 3	Rücktrittsgebühren	iptalde kesilen ücret	取消料
car hire office 7	Autoverleihbüro	araba kiralama bürosu	車賃貸事務所
card holder 9	Kartenbesitzer(in)	kart sahibi	カード保持者
cashier 9	Kassierer(in)	kasiyer/veznedar	出納係
cask 16	Faß	fıçı	樽
catamaran 8	Katamaran	çift tekneli kayık	キャタマラン（双胴船）
category 11	Kategorie	kategori	カテゴリー／範疇
cause offence 14 (US: to offend)	beleidigen	sinirlendirmek/öfkelendirmek	怒らせる
cave 17	Höhle	mağara	洞窟／洞穴
cavort 17	tollen	sıçramak	跳ねる／跳ね返る
cellar 16	Keller	mahzen	地下室（特に葡萄酒の貯蔵所）
check in (verb) 2	einchecken	giriş kaydını yaptırmak	チェック・インする
check-in (adj.) 2	Abfertigung	giriş	チェック・インの
checklist 15	Checkliste	kontrol listesi	チェックリスト／照合リスト
cheque 4 (US: check)	Scheck	çek	小切手
classroom-style 15	in Klassenzimmerform	sınıf düzeninde	教室型式（の）
client 6	Kunde/Kundin	müşteri	顧客
cliff 8	Klippe	kayalık	崖／絶壁
closed 12	geschlossen	kapalı	閉ざされて／閉めて
coastline 10	Küste	kıyı	海岸線
commission 9	Provision	komisyon	手数料
commitment 15	Engagement	kendini adama	献身／責任
complain 14	sich beschweren	şikayet etmek	苦情を申し立てる／不平を言う
complaint 14	Beschwerde	şikayet	苦情／不平
comprehensive 9	komplett	herşeyi kapsayan	包括的な
computer 2	Computer	bilgisayar	コンピューター
conference 15	Tagung	konferans	会議
confirmation 12	Bestätigung	teyid/konfirme	確認
confirmed 3	bestätigt	teyid edilmiş/konfirme edilmis	確認された
contact address 2	Kontaktadresse	bağlantı adresi	連絡場所
continental 4	europäisch	kıta Avrupasının	大陸の
contractor 15	beauftragte Firma	müteahit/taşaron	請負人
coral (adj.) 10	Korallen-	mercan	珊瑚の
cordless microphone 15	kabelloses Mikrophon	kablosuz mikrofon	コードの要らないマイクロフォン
corridor 7	Korridor	koridor	廊下
countryside 4	Landschaft	kırsal alan/köyler	田園地方
couple 11	Paar	çift	夫婦
cove 10	(kleine) Bucht	koy	入江
cover (verb) 3	decken	.....karşılığı olarak	（費用等を）償う
credit card 4	Kreditkarte	kredi kartı	クレディット・カード
cross-channel 4	Kanal-	Manş	海峡横断の
cruise 8	Kreuzfahrt	gezinti	巡行
cuisine 10	Küche	.....mutfağı	料理
culture 17	Kultur	kültür	文化／養殖／栽培
currency 9	Währung	para	通貨
customer 1	Kunde/Kundin	müşteri	顧客

Word list

ENGLISH/US ENGLISH	FRENCH	SPANISH	ITALIAN
daily 18	chaque jour	diario	giornaliero/tutti i giorni
deal with 1	traiter	tratar con	trattare/occuparsi di
delegate 15	délégué	congresista	delegato/a
delight 17	régal	(hacer) las delicias de	delizia
departure 2	départ	salida	partenza
departure lounge 7	salle d'embarquement	sala de salidas	sala d'attesa partenze
deposit 3	arrhes	depósito	deposito
destination 3	destination	destino	destinazione
dial (verb) 13	composer	marcar	chiamare (comporre il numero)
direct (adj.) 5 (US: through)	direct	directo	diretto
direct (verb) 7	diriger	dirigir	dare indicazioni a
discerning 20	judicieux	que saben lo que quieren	avveduto
discount 4	réduction	descuento	sconto
display (noun) 17	exposition	despliegue/demostración	esposizione mostra
document 14	document	documento	documento
domestic 7	intérieur	nacional	nazionale
double 11	chambre avec lit à deux places	doble	doppio/a
duration 6	durée	duración	durata
duty-free shop 7	magasin hors taxe	tienda libre de impuestos	duty-free shop
Easter 7	Pâques	Pascua	Pasqua
Economy Class 3	classe économique	Clase Económica	classe economica
employee 5	employé	empleado	dipendente
enclose 4	joindre	adjuntar	allegare
enquiry 4 (US: inquiry)	renseignement	pedir información	richiesta di informazioni
entertainment 10	distraction	diversión	divertimenti
equipment 15	matériel	equipo	attrezzatura
escalator 7	escalator	escaleras automáticas	scala mobile
establish 13	établir	crear	istituire
estate 16	(ici) département	finca	tenuta
excavations 16	fouilles	excavaciones	scavi
exchange rate 9	taux de change	tarifa de cambio	tasso di cambio
excursion 6	excursion	excursión	escursione, giro turistico
expire 9	expirer	vencerse	scadere
expiry date 2	date d'expiration	fecha de vencimiento	data di scadenza
(US: expiration date)			
explore 8	explorer	explorar	esplorare
extension 11	agrandissement d'une maison	extensión	estensione/dépendence
extraction 16	extraction	extracción	estrazione
facilities 7	installations	facilidades	servizi
family room 11	chambre familiale	habitación para familias	stanza per ospiti con bambini
FAX 6	télécopie, FAX	FAX	telefax
fermentation 16	fermentation	fermentación	fermentazione
ferry 4	ferry	ferry	traghetto
festival 16	fête	festival	festa
first floor 7	premier étage	primer piso	primo piano
(US: second floor)			
fitness centre 10	club de remise en forme	gimnasio	centro esercitazioni fisiche
(US: fitness center)			
flight 1	vol	vuelo	volo
flight number 3	numéro de vol	número de vuelo	numero di volo
flippers 19	palmes	aletas	pinne
floodlit 19	illuminé	iluminado con focos	illuminato a giorno
foreign 1	étranger	extranjero	straniero
fortnight 19 (US: two weeks)	quinze jours	quince días	quindici giorni/due settimane
front-facing 5	dans le sens de la marche	cara a la máquina	rivolto sul davanti
gesture 14	geste	gesto	gesto
give directions 7	donner des directions	indicar	dare indicazioni

ENGLISH/US ENGLISH	GERMAN	TURKISH	JAPANESE
daily 18	täglich	günlük	毎日
deal with 1	sich befassen mit	...ile iş yapmak/ ...lara hitap etmek	取り扱う
delegate 15	Delegierte(r)	delege	（派遣）代表者
delight 17	Freude	zevk/beğeni	喜び
departure 2	Abflug	kalkış	出発
departure lounge 7	Abflughalle	giden yolcu salonu	出発ラウンジ
deposit 3	Anzahlung	depozit	預託金／保証金
destination 3	Zielort	gideceği yer	目的地
dial (verb) 13	wählen	çevirmek (telefon numarası)	（電話の）ダイヤルを回す
direct (adj.) 5 (US: through)	durchgehend	direkt	直通の
direct (verb) 7	Weg sagen	yol göstermek	指示する／道を教える
discerning 20	anspruchsvoll	ince beğeniye sahip	炯眼の／認識の鋭い
discount 4	Ermäßigung	indirim	割引
display (noun) 17	Vorführung	gösteri	陳列／展示／表示
document 14	Dokument	belge/döküman	書類
domestic 7	Inland-	iç (hatlar)	国内の
double 11	Doppelzimmer	çift kişilik	ダブル／２倍の
duration 6	Dauer	süre	（滞在）持続期間
duty-free shop 7	Duty-free-shop	gümrüksüz satış mağazası	免税店

ENGLISH/US ENGLISH	GERMAN	TURKISH	JAPANESE
Easter 7	Ostern	Paskalya	イースター／復活
Economy Class 3	Touristenklasse	ekonomi mevki	エコノミー・クラス
employee 5	Angestellte(r)	çalışan	従業員
enclose 4	beifügen	ilişikte sunmak	同封する
enquiry 4 (US: inquiry)	Anfrage	bilgi alma	問合わせ
entertainment 10	Unterhaltung	eğlence	娯楽催し物
equipment 15	Ausstattung	araç-gereç	設備／装置
escalator 7	Rolltreppe	yürüyen merdiven	エスカレーター
establish 13	schaffen	kurmak	確立する
estate 16	Gut	topraklar/tarla	地所／私有地
excavations 16	Ausgrabungen	kazılar	発掘
exchange rate 9	Wechselkurs	döviz kuru	（外為）交換率
excursion 6	Ausflug	gezi/gezinti	遊覧／小旅行
expire 9	ungültig werden	süresi dolmak	有効期限が切れる
expiry date 2 (US: expiration date)	Verfallsdatum	(süre) bitiş tarihi	有効期限終了日
explore 8	erkunden	dolaşmak/araştırmak	探検する
extension 11	Anbau	ilave/genişleme	拡張
extraction 16	Entsaftung	suyunu sıkma/ekstresini alma	抽出／絞り出し

ENGLISH/US ENGLISH	GERMAN	TURKISH	JAPANESE
facilities 7	Einrichtungen	tesisler	施設／設備
family room 11	Zimmer mit Kinderbett	aile odaları	家族部屋
FAX 6	FAX	faks	ファックス
fermentation 16	Gärung	mayalanma	醸酵
ferry 4	Fähre	vapur	フェリー／渡し船
festival 16	Festspiele	festival	祭り
first floor 7 (US: second floor)	erste Etage	birinci kat	１階（欧州）＝（日本／米国の２階）
fitness centre 10 (US: fitness center)	Fitneßcenter	zayıflama salonu	フィットネス・センター
flight 4	Flug	uçuş	航空便
flight number 3	Flugnummer	uçuş numarası	航空便番号
flippers 19	Flossen	paletler	フリッパー／足ひれ
floodlit 19	unter Flutlicht	aydınlatılmış	（投光照明された）
foreign 1	ausländisch	yabancı	外国の
fortnight 19 (US: two weeks)	vierzehn Tage	onbeş gün	２週間
front-facing 5	in Fahrtrichtung	öne bakan	進行方向向きの

ENGLISH/US ENGLISH	GERMAN	TURKISH	JAPANESE
gesture 14	Geste	jest/el kol işaretleri	挙動／意志表示
give directions 7	Richtung angeben	yol tarif etmek	道順を教える

Word list

ENGLISH/US ENGLISH	FRENCH	SPANISH	ITALIAN
gondola 18	gondole	góndola	gondola
goods 7	marchandises	mercancías	merci
goodwill 14	bonne volonté	buena voluntad	buona volontà
gratuity 6	pourboire	propinas	mancia
guarantee (verb) 18	garantir	garantizar	garantire
guide-lines 12	guide (directives)	directrices	criteri
gymnasium 10	gymnase	gimnasio	palestra
hair-drier 11 (US: hair dryer)	sèche-cheveux	secador (de pelo)	fon
handicraft 8 (US: arts and crafts)	artisanat	artesanía	artigianato
handle (verb) 14	prendre en charge	manejar	trattare
heighten 12	accentuer	aumentar	accrescere
hippopotamus 16	hippopotame	hipopótamo	ippopotamo
hire (noun) 15 (US: cost)	louer	alquilar	noleggio
honeymoon 11	lune de miel	luna de miel	luna di miele
identification 13	identité	identificación	documento di identità
identity 9	identité	identidad	identità
imperial 13	impérial	imperial	imperiale
impressed 11	impressionné	impresionado	favorevolmente colpito/a
in demand 20	demandé	en demanda	richiesto
inclination 19	envies	inclinación	preferenza/inclinazione
included 4	compris	incluído	compreso
inclusive 5	compris	inclusive	compreso
incoming 12	de l'extérieur	llamada del exterior	in arrivo
inconvenience 14	désagrément	molestia	inconveniente/scomodità
inconvenient 12	inopportun	inoportuno	scomodo
informal 10	sans prétention	informal	informale
instructor 1	moniteur	instructor	istruttore
insurance 6	assurance	seguro	assicurazione
interconnecting 11 (US: adjoining)	communicant	que se comunican	comunicante
internal 6 (US: domestic)	intérieur	interno	interno
interpreter 15	interprète	intérprete	interprete
interrupt 12	interrompre	interrumpir	interrompere
interview (verb) 15	faire passer un entretien	entrevistar	tenere un colloquio con
intonation 12	intonation	entonación	inflessione/intonazione
invalid 9	non valable	inválido	non valido/invalido
invoice 6	facture	recibo	fattura
itinerary 14	itinéraire	itinerario	itinerario
jacuzzi 10	jacuzzi	jacuzzi	idromassaggio
jewellery 8 (US: jewelry)	bijoux	joyas	gioielleria
junk (boat) 8	jonque	junco (barca)	giunca
kayak 19	kayak	kayak	kayak
lake 18	lac	lago	lago
leaflet 4	brochure	folleto	opuscolo
leisurely 17	sans vous fatiguer	ocio	tranquillo
licence 6 (US: license)	permis de conduire	permiso	patente
limit 9	limite	límite	limite
locality 7	localité	localidad	zona/località
location 10	situation	situación	posizione
long-haul 20 (US: far away)	lointain	(billete) de largo recorrido	a grande distanza
lost property office 7	bureau des objets trouvés	oficina de objetos perdidos	ufficio oggetti smarriti
luggage 4	bagage	equipaje	bagaglio

ENGLISH/US ENGLISH	GERMAN	TURKISH	JAPANESE
gondola 18	Gondel	gondol	ゴンドラ
goods 7	Waren	mallar	商品
goodwill 14	Wohlwollen	iyi niyet	善意
gratuity 6	Trinkgeld	bahşiş	チップ／心付け
guarantee (verb) 18	garantieren	garantilemek	保証する
guide-lines 12	Richtlinien	kullanma kılavuzu	ガイドライン／指標
gymnasium 10	Sportraum	spor salonu/cimnastikhane	体育館
hair-drier 11 (US: hair dryer)	Haartrockner	saç kurutma makinası	ヘア・ドライヤー
handicraft 8	Kunsthandwerk	el sanatları	手工芸品
(US: arts and crafts)			ジープ
handle (verb) 14	bearbeiten	halletmek/ele almak	処理する／取り扱う
heighten 12	erhöhen	güçlendirmek/yükseltmek	高める／強める
hippopotamus 16	Nilpferd	su aygırı	河馬
hire (noun) 15 (US: cost)	Mieten	kira ücreti	賃貸料／使用料
honeymoon 11	Flitterwochen	balayı	新婚（旅行）期間
identification 13	Ausweispapiere	kimlik tespiti	同一人物である事の証明
identity 9	Identität	kimlik/hüviyet	同一人物であること
imperial 13	kaiserlich	emperyal	壮大な
impressed 11	beeindruckt	çok beğenme	印象づけられた（形容詞）
in demand 20	gefragt	talep edilmekte	需要がある
inclination 19	Neigung	zevk/eğilim	嗜好／好み／傾向
included 4	inbegriffen	içinde/dahil	含まれて（いる）
inclusive 5	inklusive	dahil/içeren	を含んだ／込みの)
incoming 12	eingehend	gelen	入って来る（形容詞）
inconvenience 14	Unannehmlichkeit	aksilik/terslik	不都合／迷惑／不便
inconvenient 12	ungelegen	elverişsiz	都合の悪い／不便な
informal 10	zwanglos	samimi ortamda	形式ばらない／堅苦しくない
instructor 1	Lehrer(in)	öğretmen	指導員／教員
insurance 6	Versicherung	sigorta	保険
interconnecting 11	miteinander verbunden	iç bağlantılı	相互連絡している（形容詞）
(US: adjoining)			
internal 6 (US: domestic)	landesintern	iç	国内の
interpreter 15	Dolmetscher(in)	tercüman/dilmaç	通訳
interrupt 12	unterbrechen	sözünü kesmek/araya girmek	邪魔をする／妨げる
interview (verb) 15	Vorstellungsgespräch führen	mülakatta bulunmak	インタビューする
intonation 12	Intonation	konuşmanın tonu/seslem	イントネーション／声の抑揚
invalid 9	ungültig	geçersiz	無効の
invoice 6	Rechnung	fatura	請求書
itinerary 14	Reiseroute	seyahat programı	旅行日程
jacuzzi 10	Brausebad	jakuze banyo	ジャクージ
jewellery 8 (US: jewelry)	Schmuck	mücevherat	貴金属装身具類
junk (boat) 8	Dschunke	Çin yelkenlisi	ジャンク（平底帆船）
kayak 19	Kajak	Eskimo kanosu	カヤック（一人乗り用小舟）
lake 18	See	göl	湖
leaflet 4	Prospekt	kısa broşür	パンフレット
leisurely 17	geruhsam	boş zamanları değerlendirme	ゆったりした／悠長な
licence 6 (US: license)	Führerschein	ehliyet	免許証
limit 9	Grenze	sınır/limit	制限（額）
locality 7	Gegend	bölge	地方／付近
location 10	Lage	ortam/yer	位置／所在場所
long-haul 20 (US: far away)	Fern-	uzun mesafe	長距離
lost property office 7	Fundbüro	kayıp eşya bürosu	紛失物取扱所
luggage 4	Gepäck	bavullar/bagaj/yük	手荷物

Word list

ENGLISH/US ENGLISH	FRENCH	SPANISH	ITALIAN
manager 3	directeur	director gerente	direttore/gestore/responsabile
marine life 10	vie marine	vida marina	vita marina
meeting room 15	salle de réunion	sala de reuniones	sala riunioni
mileage 19	kilométrage	kilometraje	chilometraggio
mini-bar 10	mini bar	mini-bar	frigobar
monastery 8	monastère	monasterio	monastero
monument 16	monument	monumento	monumento
motorway 15 (US: expressway)	autoroute	autopista	autostrada
mouthpiece 12	microphone	micrófono	imboccatura
native 10	du pays	nativo	indigeno
negotiate 11	négocier	negociar	negoziare
network 4	réseau	red	rete
nightlife 8	vie nocturne	vida nocturna	vita notturna
non-stop 2	direct	sin escalas/directo	senza scalo
oceanarium 8	marineland	acuario/oceanarium	oceanario
offer 4	offre	ofrecer	offerta
open-air 8	en plein air	al aire libre	all'aperto
operate 2	être en service	estar en funcionamiento	essere in servizio/in funzione
option 6	option	opción	opzione
organized 1	organisé	organizado	organizzato
overhead projector 15	rétro-projecteur	proyector de transparencias	lavagna luminosa
overlook 10	surplomber	tener vistas a	dominare (una vista)
package holiday 1 (US: package tour)	voyage organisé	vacaciones con todo incluído	vacanze organizzate
passenger 3	passager	pasajero	passeggero/a
passport control 7	contrôle des passeports	control de pasaporte	controllo passaporti
patio 10	patio	patio	patio
pattern 20	schéma	modelo/pauta	modello
payment 9	paiement	pago	pagamento
peak 8	sommet, pic	pico	picco/cima/vetta
personality 15	personnalité	personalidad	carattere/personalità
plain (geog.) 17	plaine	llano/llanura	pianura
pleasure 13	plaisir	placer	piacere
poolside 11	attenant à la piscine	al lado de la piscina	ai bordi della piscina
prefer 5	préférer	preferir	preferire
preference 5	préférence	preferencia	preferenza
prevent 5	éviter	prevenir	prevenire/evitare
printout 9	copie papier	impresión/printout	stampato (sost.)
priority 20	priorité	prioridad	priorità
procedure 9	règlement	trámite	procedura
process 16	procédé	proceso	processo
progress (noun) 20	progrès	progreso	progresso
prohibition 6	interdiction	prohibición	proibizione
promote 15	promouvoir	dar un ascenso	promuovere
pronunciation 12	prononciation	pronunciación	pronuncia
provisional 6 (US: unconfirmed)	provisoire	provisional	provvisorio
pursuit 19	activité	pasatiempo	attività/passatempo
pyramid 16	pyramide	pirámide	piramide
qualification 20	qualification	capacitación	requisito
quality 20	qualité	calidad	qualità
racecourse 8 (US: racetrack)	champ de course	hipódromo	ippodromo
rating 13	classement	clasificación	categoria

Word list

ENGLISH/US ENGLISH	GERMAN	TURKISH	JAPANESE
manager 3	Abteilungsleiter(in)	yönetici	マネジャー
marine life 10	Meeresfauna und -flora	deniz yaşamı	海洋生物
meeting room 15	Tagungsraum	toplantı odası	会合室
mileage 19	Meilenzahl	mil	総マイル数
mini-bar 10	Minibar	mini-bar	ミニ・バー
monastery 8	Kloster	manastır	修道院
monument 16	Denkmal	anıt	記念碑／遺跡
motorway 15 (US: expressway)	Autobahn	kara yolu (şehirlerarası)	高速道路
mouthpiece 12	Sprechmuschel	ahize	送話口
native 10	einheimisch	yerli	その土地本来の
negotiate 11	verhandeln	görüşmek/tartışmak	交渉する
network 4	Netz	ağ	ネットワーク／連絡網
nightlife 8	Nachleben	gece hayatı	夜遊び／夜の生活
non-stop 2	Nonstop-	hiç durmaksızın/hiç bir yere uğramadan	途中止まらない（直通の）
oceanarium 8	Ozeanarium	okyanus balıkları akvaryumu	海洋大水族館
offer 4	Angebot	sunmak	提供／提供する
open-air 8	im Freien	açık hava	野外の
operate 2	verkehren	(uçuşlar) yapılacaktır	運行する
option 6	Option	opsiyon/tercih	オプション／選択権
organized 1	geplant	düzenlenmiş/organize edilmiş	計画準備されて（いる）
overhead projector 15	Overheadprojektor	tepegöz	オーヴァーヘッド・プロジェクター
overlook 10	überblicken	...manzarası olmak/... e bakar	見渡す／見晴らす
package holiday 1 (US: package tour)	Pauschalreise	paket tatil turu	パッケージ・ホリデー（運賃宿泊費等一切込みの休日旅行）
passenger 3	Reisende(r)	yolcu	旅客／乗客
passport control 7	Paßkontrolle	pasaport kontrolü	旅券管理（所）
patio 10	Veranda	avlu/veranda/teras	パチオ（庭の家寄りに食事喫茶のできるようにしたテラス）
pattern 20	Muster	model	様式／パターン
payment 9	Zahlung	ödeme	支払い
peak 8	Gipfel	doruk/tepe	山頂
personality 15	Persönlichkeit	kişilik	性格／個性
plain (geog.) 17	Ebene	ova	平原／大草原
pleasure 13	Vergnügen	hoşnutluk/zevk	喜び
poolside 11	am Beckenrand	havuz kenarı	プールの側の
prefer 5	vorziehen	tercih etmek	寧ろ一の方を好む／取る
preference 5	Präferenz	tercih/seçim	好ましい方を選ぶこと
prevent 5	verhindern	önlemek	避ける／防ぐ
printout 9	Ausdruck	yazılı dökümü	配付用印刷物
priority 20	Priorität	öncelik	優先権
procedure 9	Verfahrensweise	prosedür/izlenen yol	手続き／手順
process 16	Prozeß	süreç	工程／過程
progress (noun) 20	Fortschritte	terfi	進展／発展
prohibition 6	Verbot	yasaklama	禁止
promote 15	werben für	tanıtmak	促進する／宣伝する
pronunciation 12	Aussprache	teleffuz	発音
provisional 6 (US: unconfirmed)	provisorisch	geçici/önkayıt	仮の／暫定的の
pursuit 19	Freizeitbeschäftigung	faaliyet/etkinlik	追求／遂行／楽しみ
pyramid 16	Pyramide	piramit	ピラミッド
qualification 20	Qualifikation	nitelikler	資格
quality 20	Qualität	nitelik/kalite	品質
racecourse 8 (US: racetrack)	Rennbahn	hipodrom	競馬場／競争場
rating 13	Klasse	sınıflandırma	格付け／等級

Word list

ENGLISH/US ENGLISH	FRENCH	SPANISH	ITALIAN
raw 18	cru	crudo	crudo
rear-facing 5	dans le sens inverse de la marche	de espaldas a la máquina	rivolto sul dietro
receipt 9	reçu	recibo	ricevuta
reception (hotel) 9 (US: front desk)	réception	recepción	ricezione (d'albergo)
receptionist 13	réceptioniste	recepcionista	addetto/a alla ricezione
recommend 4	recommander	recomendar	consigliare
reduced rate 4	prix réduit	tarifa reducida	tariffa ridotta
refined 13	raffiné	elegante	raffinato
refreshments 5	refraîchissements	refrescos	bevande e spuntini
refund (verb) 14	rembourser	reembolsar	rimborsare
relationship 14	relation	relación	rapporto
rental 19	location	alquiler	noleggio
report to 20	dépendre de	dar cuentas a/informar a	dipendere da
representative 1	responsable	representante	rappresentante
reputation 8	réputation	reputación	fama/reputazione
request 4	demande	pedido/solicitud/ruego	richiesta
requirement 6	exigence	requisito	necessità/fabbisogno
research (noun) 20	enquête	estudios	ricerca
reservation 2	réservation	reserva	prenotazione
resort 6	lieu de vacances	centro de veraneo	stazione (località) di soggiorno
restriction 2	restriction	restricción	restrizione
retailer 20	(ici) agence de voyages	minorista	(qui) agenzia di viaggi
return (ticket) 2 (US: round-trip)	aller retour	de ida y vuelta	(biglietto di) andata e ritorno
riding 19	équitation	montar a caballo	equitazione
round-the-world 2	autour du monde	alrededor del mundo	per il giro del mondo
rubber 16	caoutchouc	goma	gommo
ruins 16	ruines	ruinas	rovine
safari 16	safari	safari	safari
satisfactory 14	satisfaisant	satisfactorio	soddisfacente
sauna 10	sauna	sauna	sauna
scenery 17	scène	paisaje	paesaggio
screen 15	écran	pantalla	schermo
scuba diving 1	plongée sous-marine	submarinismo/bucear	immersioni subacquee (con cilindro)
seafood 10	fruits de mer	mariscos	frutti di mare/pesce commestibile
season (holiday) 11	saison	temporada	stagione
second-rate 20	de deuxième choix	de segunda clase	di second'ordine
selective 20	sélectif	selectivo	selettivo
self-catering 20	organisation individuelle des repas	con facilidades para cocinar	dove si può cucinare autonomamente
seminar 15	séminaire	seminario	seminario
serenade 18	sérénade	serenata	serenata
settle an account 18	solder un compte	saldar la cuenta	saldare un conto
shaded 13	ombragé	con sombra	ombreggiato
shark 13	requin	tiburón	pescecane/squalo
signature 9	signature	firma	firma
silversmith 17	orfèvre	platero	argentiere
single (ticket) 4 (US: one-way)	aller simple	de ida	(biglietto di) solo andata
sleeper 5	couchette	coche-cama	vagone letto/wagon lit
slope 17	pente	pendiente	pendio
snake 18	serpent	serpiente	serpente
snorkelling 19	plongée avec masque et tuba	bucear	immersioni subacquee (con respiratore
solarium 11	solarium	solarium	solarium
souvenir 17	souvenir	souvenir	souvenir/ricordo
sports complex 10	complexe sportif	polideportivo	complesso sportivo
squash 8	squash	squash	squash
stairs 7	escalier	escaleras	scala/scale
stall 8 (US: stand)	échoppe	puesto/caseta	bancarella
standard 13	standard	nivel/estándar	livello
stopover 2	halte	escala	scalo intermedio

ENGLISH/US ENGLISH	GERMAN	TURKISH	JAPANESE
raw 18	roh	çiğ	生の
rear-facing 5	gegen die Fahrtrichtung	arkaya bakan	進行方向とは逆向きの
receipt 9	Quittung	makbuz/alındı makbuzu	領収書
reception (hotel) 9 (US: front desk)	Empfang	resepsiyon/kabul bürosu	受付
receptionist 13	Empfangschef/Empfangsdame	resepsiyon memuru	受付係
recommend 4	empfehlen	tavsiye etmek/salık vermek	推薦する
reduced rate 4	ermäßigter Preis	indirimli fiyat	割引率
refined 13	vornehm	rafine/incelikli	洗練されて（いる）
refreshments 5	(kleine) Erfrischungen	yiyecek-içecekler	軽食／飲物
refund (verb) 14	zurückerstatten	geri ödemek	払い戻す
relationship 14	Beziehung	ilişki	関係／関連
rental 19	Verleih	kiralama	レンタル／賃貸
report to 20	Bericht erstatten	bağlı olma/sorumlu olma	に報告する
representative 1	Vertreter(in)	temsilci	代表者
reputation 8	Ruf	ün/şöhret	名声／評判
request 4	Bitte/Wunsch	istek	要請（する）
requirement 6	Bedürfnis	ihtiyaç	必要条件
research (noun) 20	Forschung	araştırma	研究／調査
reservation 2	Reservierung	yer ayırtma/rezervasyon	予約
resort 6	Urlaubsort	yazlık	リゾート／行楽地
restriction 2	Einschränkung	kısıtlama	制限
retailer 20	(hier) Reisebüro	perakendeci	小売業者
return (ticket) 2 (US: round-trip)	Rückfahrschein	gidiş-dönüş (bileti)	往復（切符）
riding 19	Reiten	ata binme	馬術
round-the-world 2	Weltrundreise-	dünya turu	世界周遊
rubber 16	Kautschuk	kauçuk	ゴム
ruins 16	Ruinen	harabeler	遺跡
safari 16	Safari	safari	サファリ／探検旅行
satisfactory 14	befriedigend	tatmin edici/yeterli	満足すべき
sauna 10	Sauna	sauna/fin hamamı	サウナ
scenery 17	Landschaft	manzara	風景
screen 15	Leinwand	ekran	スクリーン
scuba diving 1	Sporttauchen	tüple dalma	スキューバ・ダイビング
seafood 10	Meeresfrüchte	deniz ürünleri	海産食物
season (holiday) 11	Saison	sezon/mevsim	季節
second-rate 20	zweitklassig	ikinci sınıf	二流の／低級な
selective 20	wählerisch	seçici	選択的な／選り好みする
self-catering 20	für Selbstversorger	kendi yiyecek ihtiyacını karşılama	食事を自分で賄う（形容詞）
seminar 15	Seminar	seminer	セミナー
serenade 18	Serenade	serenad	セレナード／小夜曲
settle an account 18	Konto ausgleichen	hesabı halletmek	勘定を済ませる／支払う
shaded 13	im Schatten	gölgeli	日陰の
shark 13	Haifisch	köpek balığı	鮫／フカ
signature 9	Unterschrift	imza	署名
silversmith 17	Silberschmied	gümüş üstüne çalışan kuyumcu	銀細工師
single (ticket) 4 (US: one-way)	einfach	gidiş (bileti)	片道（切符）
sleeper 5	Schlafwagen	yataklı (vagon)	寝台車
slope 17	Hang	yamaç	傾斜／勾配
snake 18	Schlange	yılan	蛇
snorkelling 19	schnorcheln	şnorkel	スノーケルを水面に出して潜行する
solarium 11	Solarium	solaryum/güneş banyosu camekanı	日光浴室
souvenir 17	Andenken	hatıra (eşya)	記念品／土産品
sports complex 10	Sportanlage	spor tesisleri	複合スポーツ競技場
squash 8	Squash	kapalı yerde raketle oyanan bir top oyunu	スクオッシュ
stairs 7	Treppe	merdivenler	階段
stall 8 (US: stand)	Stand	tezgah	屋台店／露店
standard 13	Standard	standard	水準／標準
stopover 2	Zwischenstation	...a uğramak	ストップ・オーヴァー（飛行機旅行での途中下車）

Word list

ENGLISH/US ENGLISH	FRENCH	SPANISH	ITALIAN
street map 7	plan (de rues)	mapa de la ciudad	carta stradale
stroll 8	se promener	paseo	passeggiare
substandard 20	de mauvaise qualité	inferior al nivel normal	di livello inferiore
suite 11	suite	suite/habitaciones	appartamento (d'albergo)
summary 15	résumé	resumen	riassunto
supervisor 14	responsable	supervisor	supervisore
supplement 9 (US: surcharge)	supplément	suplemento	supplemento
surfboard 19	surf	tabla de surf	tavola da surf
syndicate room 15	salle de réunion	sala de reuniones	sala riunioni piccola
(US: conference room)			
tariff 9	tarif	tarifa	tariffa
tavern 17	taverne	taberna	taverna
tax-free 7	hors taxe	libre de impuestos	non gravato da tasse
telex 2	télex	telex	telex
temple 16	temple	templo	tempio
terminal 7	terminal	terminal	terminale
theatre-style 15	style salle de théâtre	estilo teatro	tipo sala cinematografica
timetable 2	horaires	horario	orario
tour guide 1	guide touristique	guía turístico	guida turistica
traditional 13	traditionnel	tradicional	tradizionale
tram 8 (US: streetcar)	tramway, tram	tranvía	tram
transaction 9	transaction	transacción	transazione
transfer (noun) 6	transfert	traslado	trasferimento
travel agency 1	agence de voyages	agencia de viajes	agenzia di viaggi
travel clerk 2 (US: travel agent)	employé d'une agence de voyages	empleado de oficina de viajes	impiegato/a (al banco viaggi)
travel consultant 20	conseiller de voyages	consultor de turismo	consulente di viaggi
trek 20	randonnée	caminata/excursión	lungo viaggio a tappe
tunnel 16	tunnel	túnel	tunnel/galleria
twin-bedded 6	avec lits jumeaux	de dos camas	a due letti
unique 13	unique	único	unico, singolare
unlimited 4	illimité	sin restricciones	illimitato
upgrade 14	surclasser	subir de categoría	cambiare (migliorare/valorizzare)
vacancy 20	poste vacant	cuarto vacante	posto di lavoro disponibile
valid 9	valable	válido	valido
vathouse 16	pressoir	vinería	deposito dei tini
Venetian 18	vénitien	veneciano	veneziano/a
venue 15 (US: locale)	lieu de rendez-vous	local	sede/luogo
via 3	via	vía	via/passando per
video recorder 15 (US: VCR)	magnétoscope	videograbadora	videoregistratore
visa 6	visa	visado	visto
volumes (sales) 20	(ici) nombre de	cantidad	volumi (vendite)
water-skiing 19	ski nautique	esquí acuático	sci d'acqua
waterfront 8	front de mer	muelles	lungomare
watersports 11	sports nautiques	deportes acuáticos/naúticos	sport acquatici
weekend break 11	week end d'évasion	fin de semana	piccola vacanza di fine settimana
welcome (verb) 1	accueillir	dar la bienvenida	dare il benvenuto
well (noun) 16	puits	pozo	pozzo
whale 17	baleine	ballena	balena
wildlife 16	vie sauvage	fauna	animali selvatici
windsurfing 1	planche à voile	hacer tabla/windsurf	surf a vela
wine 16	vin	vino	vino
wooden 16	en bois	de madera	di legno
woods 18	bois (forêt)	bosques	bosco, boschi

ENGLISH/US ENGLISH	GERMAN	TURKISH	JAPANESE
street map 7	Straßenplan	şehir planı	街路地図
stroll 8	herumspazieren	gezmek	散歩（する）／ぶらつく
substandard 20	minderwertig	standardın altında	標準以下の
suite 11	Suite	süit	スウィート（2間以上の1続きの部屋）
summary 13	Zusammenfassung	özel	摘要／概略
supervisor 14	Aufsicht	süpervizör/denetçi	監督者
supplement 9 (US: surcharge)	Zuschlag	ilave ücret	追加
surfboard 19	Surfbrett	sörf (tahtası)	サーフボード
syndicate room 15 (US: conference room)	Seminarraum	toplantı odası	会合室
tariff 9	Tarif	ücret tarifesi	料金（表）
tavern 17	Taverne	taverna/meyhane	居酒屋／宿屋
tax-free 7	zollfrei	gümrükten muaf	免税の
telex 2	Fernschreiben	teleks	テレックス
temple 16	Tempel	tapınak	神殿／寺院
terminal 7	Terminal	terminal	ターミナル
theatre-style 15	in Hörsaalform	konferans düzeni	劇場型式（の）
timetable 2	Flugplan	tarife (uçak/tren/otobüs)	時間表
tour guide 1	Reiseführen(in)	tur rehberi	観光ガイド
traditional 13	traditionell	geleneksel	伝統的な
tram 8 (US: streetcar)	Straßenbahn	tramvay	市街電車
transaction 9	Abwicklung	işlem/muamele	取引
transfer (noun) 6	Transfer	ulaşım	移動
travel agency 1	Reisebüro	seyahat acentası	旅行代理店
travel clerk 2 (US: travel agent)	Reisebüroangestellte(r)	seyahat acentası görevlisi	旅行代理店事務員
travel consultant 20	Reiseberater(in)	seyahat danışmanı	旅行コンサルタント
trek 20	Treck	yaya yolculuk	徒歩旅行
tunnel 16	Tunnel	tünel	トンネル
twin-bedded 6	Zweibett-	cift yataklı	ツイン・ベッドの
unique 13	einzigartig	eşsiz	独特な
unlimited 4	unbegrenzt	sınırsız sayıda	無制限な
upgrade 14	verbessern	uzatmak/daha iyisini yapmak	格上げする
vacancy 20	offene Stelle	bos kadro	欠員
valid 9	gültig	gecerli	有効の
vathouse 16	Kellerei	şaraphane sarnıcı	ワイン醸造所
Venetian 18	venezianisch	Venedik	ヴェニスの
venue 15 (US: locale)	Zusammenkunftsort	toplantı yeri	行事会議の開催指定地
via 3	über	üzerinden/yoluyla	一経由
video recorder 15 (US: VCR)	Videogerät	video kayıt cihazı	ビデオ・レコーダー
visa 6	Visum	vize	査証
volumes (sales) 20	Umsätze	miktar/hacim	（売上）量
water-skiing 19	Wasserskilaufen	su kayağı	水上スキー
waterfront 8	am Wasser entlang	rıhtım	海岸通り／川、湖、海に接した土地
watersports 11	Wassersport	su sporları	ウォーター・スポーツ
weekend break 11	Wochenendurlaub	haftasonu tatili	週末の休暇
welcome (verb) 1	willkommen heißen	karşılamak	歓迎する／ようこそ　いらっしゃい
well (noun) 16	Brunnen	kuyu	井戸
whale 17	Walfisch	balina	鯨
wildlife 16	Tierwelt	vahşi yaşam	野生生物
windsurfing 1	Windsurfing	sörf	ウインド・サーフィン
wine 16	Wein	şarap	葡萄酒
wooden 16	Holz-	tahta	木製の
woods 18	Wald	orman/koru	林

Oxford University Press
Great Clarendon Street, Oxford OX2 6DP

Oxford New York
Auckland Bangkok Buenos Aires Cape Town
Chennai Dar es Salaam Delhi Hong Kong Istanbul
Karachi Kolkata Kuala Lumpur Madrid Melbourne
Mexico City Mumbai Nairobi São Paulo Shanghai
Taipei Tokyo Toronto

Oxford and *Oxford English* are trade marks
of Oxford University Press

ISBN 0 19 437602 8

© Oxford University Press 1991

First published 1991
Eleventh impression 2003

Phototypeset in New Baskerville and Gills Sans by
Tradespools Ltd.

Printed in Hong Kong.

ACKNOWLEDGEMENTS

The authors and publishers would like to thank the
following for their advice and assistance in the
preparation of this course:

The teaching staffs of the following institutions:

France
Lycée Jean Lurçat, Paris
Institut des Métiers de l'Hôtellerie et de la Restauration,
  Paris
Institut Supérieur de Tourisme, Paris
Ecole Française de Tourisme, Paris
Ecole Nationale de Commerce, Paris

Italy
Istituto Tecnico per il Turismo 'Marco Polo', Florence
Istituto Tecnico per il Turismo 'Pasolini', Milan
Istituto Professionale per il Turismo 'Caselli', Siena

Spain
Instituto de Formación Profesional, La Elipa
Vox School of Tourism, Madrid
Escuela Oficial de Turismo, Casa de Campo

Air France
Biological Journeys, California, USA
British Rail
British Tourist Authority
Club Mediterranée SA
Cox and Kings Travel Ltd, London
French Railways — SNCF
INEM, Madrid
Randolph Hotel, Oxford
Thomas Cook
Venice Simplon-Orient Express
Westminster College, London
York College of Arts and Technology: Dept of
  Community Studies
Yorkshire and Humberside Tourist Association

For permission to reproduce photographs

Boys Syndication
Mike Brett Photography
The J Allan Cash Photolibrary
Bruce Coleman
Colorific Photo Library/G. Benson
Jane Duff
James Davies Travel Photography
Greg Evans Photo Library
© Heathrow Visions 1989
Libby Howells
Impact Photos
Intasun Holidays
The International Stock Exchange Photolibrary
Japan National Tourist Organization
Melrose Film Productions Ltd
Marilyn and Garry O'Brien
Orient-Express Hotels
Tessa Pellow
Planet Earth Pictures
Queens Moat House PLC
Sefton Photo Library
Spectrum Colour Library
Swiss National Tourist Office
World Pictures/Feature-Pix Colour Library Ltd

Studio photography by Marilyn & Garry O'Brien

Location photography by Rob Judges

Illustrations by Axel Scheffler

Special thanks to Jeanne Tichbon and the staff of Oxford
Travel Agency, Oxford, for all their help and assistance.